Painting
outside the lines

Painting
outside the lines

The Life of Psychic Artist

MELISSA HARRIS

MELISSA HARRIS ART ENTERPRISES
WEST HURLEY, NEW YORK

Published in the United States by Creatrix
Distributed by: Melissa Harris Art Enterprises
PO Box 56
West Hurley, NY 12491 USA
845 340 9632 info@melissaharris.com
MelissaHarris.com

ISBN -13: 978-0-9814682-1-1
ISBN -10: 0-9814682-1-7

First Edition 2012
MelissaHarris.com

Cover image: Melissa Harris Self Portrait, 2012, Oil on Canvas, 20" x 24"
Illustrations and Artwork: © Melissa Harris, unless otherwise indicated in the image caption.

Project development/Editor: Ja-lene Clark, GatherInsight.com
Editors: Jo Ann Deck, Joann Sprott
Designer: Ja-lene Clark

PRINTED IN CHINA

CONTENTS

Introduction   9

The Psychic Child—Why Am I Different?   19
Beyond the Canvas: The Empathic Artist   28

Young Adulthood   35
*Beyond the Canvas: Atmospheres—Where to Live,
Eat, Paint   40*

NYC—Life in a Faster Lane   49
Beyond the Canvas: Teaching and Learning   56

Nomadic Whispers and Volatile Relationships   65
Beyond the Canvas: Why Women?   70

Polaroids and Crystal Balls   81
*Beyond the Canvas: The Spaces In Between—
My Comfort Zone   86*

Portrait Painting— Doorways into Souls   93
Beyond the Canvas: In the Eye of the Beholder   100

Life in France—Speaking in Tongues   107
*Beyond the Canvas: Cats and Butterflies—
Painting What I Love   116*

Hands-On Healing—Studying Energy Healing   125
  Beyond the Canvas: An Artist in Dreamtime   130

On the Road—The Sensitive Traveler   137
  Beyond the Canvas: Inspiration and Style   144

Making a Living as an Artist   155
  *Beyond the Canvas: Spirit Essence Portraits
  and Healing   162*

Day Job—Psychic Reader   173
  Beyond the Canvas: Spirit Guides   176

Is It Worth It?—Sacrifice   183
  Beyond the Canvas: About Empowerment   190

Bonus Section   194
  *12 Tips To Open the Door To Your
  Psychic and Creative Self   194*
  *The Artist and the Ego:
  Using Rejection as a Catalyst   198*
  A Few Other Favorite Paintings   201
  Visual Art Listing   209

DEDICATION

*For all those who feel that itch to create and
don't know how to move forward—may
Spirit light your way.*

INTRODUCTION

When people began to ask for a book of my artwork, I wondered what I would say. My initial thought was that the images speak for themselves; however, the more I thought about writing, the more I wanted to share. In thinking of what folks have been interested in knowing about me, I come back to three common questions:

* Does being psychic have an affect on my artwork?
* What's it like to be psychic?
* How is my world different?

I've addressed these questions in a book that is autobiographical in nature and also contains what I believe to be truths about some general traits of artists, as well as common ingredients of an artist's life.

Artists are healers, and artists are in turn healed by the act of making their art, in whatever form that art takes. As artists, we take what's out there in our crazy world and form it into a visual statement. Our role is to be commentators for the world around us. I suppose this role is a piece of our karmic task. Haven't we learned tremendous amounts by the art that each society of creatives has left behind?

My artistic statements tend to be more personal. If I don't get them up and out of me and onto the canvas I could become sick. That's just the way of it. I can only go so long before I am so filled up with emotion that I need to get it out. I'm not sure if emotion is the right word, but it's as close as I can come to describing a feeling of building up something that needs a release. At the end of a painting session, provided I have been able to stay at my craft for as long as I need to, I am sated, complete, satisfied in a way that is similar to the way one might feel after having sex. Then I can go for the next period of time until I need another release. When I walk into the studio and get a whiff of the fumes—I am elated, relieved, I am home, at least for the next few hours. While I am creating, I'm able to close off the left brain (analytical side) so that I can relax into the right brain (receptive side) and receive what needs to be captured by the paint. I observe the same sense of fulfillment in my students at the end of one of my art-making workshops. Doctors, lawyers and financial advisors learn to seek refuge in the right sides of their brains upon entering my classes.

Painting is my medicine. I had not thought of painting in those specific terms until I went on a Vision Quest in the woods of New Hampshire under the supervision of Mary Thunder (otherwise known as simply Thunder). She is a Native American peace elder that I studied with for some years. Thunder allowed me to take my watercolors while Vision Questing because she said it was my medicine. Now that I look back, the art I created in my twenties, thirties and forties is how I tended to work out or process through very literal pictorials, events and relationships occurring in my life. I painted out my pain and my yearnings with no intention of showing this art to anyone; I simply needed the release. These artistic statements were not always pleasant.

At times some of my pieces may provoke or disturb some viewers, but as they do my hope is that they may open the gateway to an unknown or dormant side of a person, one where their true power resides. I want to express how our con-

Melissa at Altar During Ceremony, c. 1995

sciousness is far more expansive than our intellect. Real pain comes from places where we split from ourselves, which are the true states of being that we need to accept without judging.

The sensual, familiar feel of buttery paint applied to surface delights me. It's what I know. I've been making that gesture since I was eleven years old. A new tube of paint, a blank canvas, primed and sanded down, ready to go—these things can make my mouth water as much as a good bar of dark chocolate. Add to that mix a new paintbrush that I have not yet mutilated by years of scrubbing excitedly over a dense surface, and I'm in paradise. The colors, my Goddess—the colors alone—how could they not make anyone happy? I am greedy for color. I have the freedom, the right to select any color I choose and place it where I like. I observe when I cannot get enough of a certain color and then apply it as liberally as I like. I have gone through decades of using one color predominantly, and then for no understandable reason, I will suddenly want to move into a different predominant color. In my early years as an artist my colors were darker and more subdued. In recent years I have selected increasingly lighter as well as more intense color. My subject matter also continues to change.

I am in the same trance or semi-trance state

when I am tuning in to do a psychic reading or when I am painting. Connecting with the core of my being, higher self, spirit guides, Source itself makes me more peaceful, so I am able to access whatever it is I may need to visit in order to bring forth my creations. For example, if I want to evoke a particular mood in a piece, I clear my mind (and meditation is most helpful for this), then transport myself to that particular scenario or one that is of a similar nature. My connection to Source coupled with my years of study in traditional artistic techniques has helped me to transmit the power of my emotions into my paintings, and that is important to me.

I didn't have children; my paintings are my children, but I don't grieve when they leave the nest. Knowing that I have brought beauty or inspiration into another's life on a daily basis is very gratifying. I can draw from an endless source of creativity, so there is always the next painting. Through these decades of a sometimes erratic and ever-evolving life, painting has been the one constant. Relationships and homes have come and gone, but my paintbox is always with me.

The Blessing Tree

She went up there to be alone,
         to be upside down,
or to hang Free.
That tree knew her
better than anyone.

The Blessing Tree, CREATRIX Publishing Line,
1992, Oil on Paper, 16" x 20"

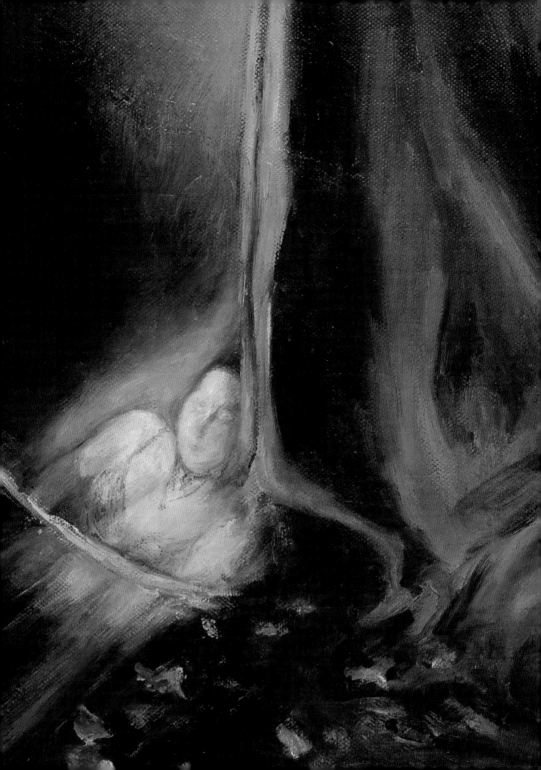

THE PSYCHIC CHILD

Why Am I Different?

As a child, my parents fed me with a steady supply of paper and crayons to keep me both still and quiet. We lived in a rural neighborhood surrounded by woods and creeks with easy access to empty fields. I loved being outside. My parents did

Early Butterfly Art by Melissa, c. 1958

not always get along well, and I needed to remove myself from the tension. To escape, I grabbed my art supplies and set myself up in nature to "color."

Making art started out partially as an escape, and throughout my life art has continued to be my medicine, my shelter in a storm. I tied a basket to a tree in the yard of our small home in Petersburg, Virginia and lifted up all the necessary items for survival for an afternoon spent up high in the trees. My survival gear included art supplies, cookies stolen from the pantry at opportune times, and a stray grey cat that was not allowed in the house. The message accompanying one of the images from my greeting card line was inspired from these memories:

She went up there to be alone, to be upside down, or to hang Free. That tree knew her better than anyone.

Melissa With Her Mother Sally, c. 1959

My mother would always say to me, "You're too sensitive;" hence my need for the tree retreat. Although my mother was quite psychic herself, she didn't realize the impact that my surroundings had on me, including any fighting between her and my father. I've always been a "psychic sponge," which makes it difficult at times to live in the world. I also came to realize that I knew things that others didn't but I didn't know why.

EARLY ATTRACTION TO THE MYSTERIOUS

The two-hour drive from our home in Petersburg to my maternal grandmother Lily's in Norfolk, Virginia on many weekends involved passing through the Dismal Swamp, whose name alone intrigued me. After watching a television special about the mysteries of this swamp, enveloped as it was in the magical imagery of tangled vines with huge roots from the trees rising up from the murky waters, I held attentive vigil in anticipation of what could be lurking there. It was during one of those journeys past the swamp that I remember my first vivid psychic experience. We passed a house with a long, narrow tree-lined drive leading up to the white wooden fence that was exactly like the house I had seen in my dreams the night before. When I shared this, my parents found it interesting but

Melissa, c. 1959

didn't make a big deal out of it. They had grown accustomed to listening to me share my active dream life. I, on the other hand, knew this to be significant.

On Saturday afternoons, when we weren't outdoors building forts or engaged in other important ventures, a friend and I loved watching Frankenstein or Mummy shows. The mysterious atmospheres in these shows attracted me. Later series like the *Twilight Zone* and the *Outer Limits* had me hooked. Because of my sensitivities to the energies of an environment, I found it fascinating to visit older homes. We had a neighbor who welcomed me over for cookies. Because I am clairsentient, I loved wandering around her house because it was full of antiques, and I could pick up on the energies thrown off by these objects. I left there in an excited, dreamy state but didn't know why. The same state of mind would occur when my mother took me to a dressmaker to hem my always too-long dresses. The seamstress was an ancient woman with a big white bun. Her home too was dark and full of antiques. Though I hated being taken away from

Dad Donald, Melissa, Mother Sally, c. 1960

nature to stand still for fittings, I loved absorbing the energy from the objects in her old southern home. My mother preferred new things, so being in old environments such as these was exotic, like visiting another country.

MY NATURE

Spirit was always with me, in a way, driving me. I knew I was different. It was difficult to understand that I had a sight and a knowing that those around me did not seem to have. I didn't know what this heightened awareness was for, or what to do with it, nor did I like being different. A child's nature is to want to fit in. There was a certain irony to being born in a rural Southern community with this psychic ability, and furthermore, to be raised in a slightly practicing Jewish family. This meant that I was *always* out of place.

Nature provided comfort as well as escape. I liked to get up really early before anyone else and go outside to listen to the birds and absorb the smells and light of the early hours. When I felt like painting I would set up a place in the yard with a little umbrella for the sun and do my drawings of horses and dancers outside. That is still how I "go to church."

PSYCHIC TEENAGER—ANY PARENT'S NIGHTMARE

Beginning around the seventh grade, maybe earlier, anything that vaguely smelled of the esoteric drew me in like a magnet. During slumber parties my friends and I consulted the Ouija board and received enough responses to believe that we had succeeded in connecting with those who had crossed over. I grew interested in the concept of what happens after death.

Melissa with Boyfriend Mickey, c. 1970

True to my nature to this day, I was not part of any one clique. I hung around with groups from the popular preppy types to the "hoods or greasers" because I loved learning about what made folks tick. This time in my life was particularly uncomfortable because of the cruelty that teenagers bestow upon each other. Being the empath that I am meant that I experienced the hurt feelings experienced by the targets of bullies. When I stuck up for those who were being picked on, I was abandoned by the "cool people."

During this time my tendency to enjoy life "on the edge" first surfaced. I was hanging around with an older, faster crowd and thrived on the adventures of fast cars, drinking, and drugs. My intuitive gifts kept me safe from harm since I could usually sense danger from a place, situation or individual and my vivid imagination provided the elaborate stories that explained my whereabouts to my parents.

Invocation Photo Study (top),
Invocation, c. 1982, Oil on Canvas, 36" x 28"

THE EMPATHIC ARTIST
Beyond the Canvas

There is an awareness that sensitives like me have that can be both a blessing and a curse. Why, you ask, is it a curse? It means for me that I can't handle being in crowds; the energy is far too much. It means that as an empath I feel in my own body the energies of other people, and if there are energies present that are less than desirable, I have to expend more of my own energy to shield myself.

The positive side of being an empath is related to painting in that I am able to easily receive energetic information from whatever subject I choose to focus on, whether that be a person, animal, plant or even a simple interior. As a child I just never understood how those around me could not see or feel what was obvious to me. Even though I am a visual artist, I don't easily see auras, what I do is feel what the other is feeling. For example, once when I was tuning into a client's past life where they had burned to death I started sweating profusely and had to stop the reading. This was one of the reasons I decided to study formally before continuing any readings. I needed to learn about shielding and protection.

My connection to Source, Spirit or my guides is important to me. Because I am empathic it is particularly important for me to stay connected to the presence of the Divine in my life. I am not concerned with who is communicating to me or what I should call this guidance; my focus is not on the messenger, it is on the message. To stay connected, I make it a practice to talk with Source or Spirit and my guides every morning first thing upon waking and last thing before I go to sleep. In the morning, I call out for assistance on what I want my day to look like. During this time I focus on what I may need help with or what I want to create and then let myself see what forms in that nothingness.

Before I go to sleep, I summon my helpers again to ask for help in dreamtime with any situation that may be up for me.

Dream Angel

She woke up with a sweet feeling
that she was loved & protected.

CREATRIX Publishing Line, c. 1997, Watercolor, 9" x 12"

Sing Out

*"After the excitement of discovering
life outside the rural South,
there was no turning back."*

Sing Out, 2010, Oil on Canvas, 18" x 24"

YOUNG ADULTHOOD

My parents were concerned (with good reason) about my ability to make a living for myself. They were sure that I would marry, have children, and not need a career, but just in case, I went to college. If I were to follow the artistic path they predicted a life surrounded by "crazy types like other artists, musicians and theater people" which proved accurate and very fulfilling.

EDUCATING AN ARTIST WITH NOMADIC TENDENCIES

The University of Virginia (UVA) was the first of five colleges I attended in a four-year roving educational experience culminating in a BFA in Painting (not one of the more practical majors one could choose in a college education). There were

Melissa with Her Cat Jupiter, c. 1984

reasons for the numerous learning institutions, but I consistently felt out of place, different, a continuation of my childhood. At least at this point in life I had a choice to stay or go.

After the excitement of discovering life outside the rural South, there was no turning back. *I wanted to know everything that was out there.* This desire may, I suppose, exist in my DNA. My paternal grandfather was a waiter on trains that traveled throughout the USA, and like me he craved the adventure of the road.

I understood quickly at the University of Virginia that I could not fit into the prevailing fraternity/sorority, good ole boy environment. After two years of attempting to find a way to exist in that world and learning that the UVA art department was not the strongest, I decided to move to Baltimore and took summer classes at the Maryland Institute of Art. I loved the Institute but wasn't crazy about Baltimore and soon after transferred to Virginia Commonwealth University (VCU) in Richmond to major in Fashion Design. I gave Fashion Design my best shot but every time the elevator passed the third floor and I caught a whiff of the oil paints and turpentine, my heart called me to ask that I give my all to painting. I was also intimidated by the math involved in the pattern-making classes, so I gave in to my yearning for the familiar sensual feel of paint to canvas and switched to a major in Painting.

I was mugged while at VCU, which left me less than enthusiastic about living in cities. After this vicious mugging, I was terrified to go out at night alone for the next two or three years. I learned to use my fine-tuned psychic antennae to search out danger. Living in Manhattan (years later) helped me to move past my fears, but due to my extreme sensitivity I continue to feel ill at ease in situations where I pick up negative or angry energies.

Next stop was an unlikely place (for an out-of-the-box type like me)—Athens, Georgia for a brief quarter of a semester at the University of Georgia. After Georgia, I was happy to pack up and head to Syracuse University for the last stop of my five-college tour in four years. I wanted to spread my wings in every sense of the word, and the South, bless its heart, tends to resist change.

I finally found "home" in the fine arts building at Syracuse. I fell hard and fast with not only the exposure to the arts in general, but for a young fellow painter named Gary who had a love and knowledge of jazz as well as the art scene of the 60s and 70s. I'd like to rationalize his addictions to drink and drug on what I could suggest was a collective, popular love for altering one's consciousness at that point in history, but if I am to be completely honest it was more than that. Gary and I were to be in an on again/off again relationship for fourteen years.

I arrived late in the semester and a half that I spent at Syracuse University. There were no studios left, but that did not deter me. I stored my paints in someone else's studio at night and dragged them out and set up my entire situation, complete with fabric backgrounds, makeshift painting table and easel each day. Later when I was attending the New York Studio school in the Village I did a series of paintings of the teeny closet in my apartment that served as a bathroom. There was a hole in the ceiling and I could see into the bathroom upstairs. Fortunately the upstairs tenant and I were destined to become life-long friends. I still don't know how I was able to manage getting an easel into the very narrow hallway to create those paintings.

Melissa with Boyfriend Gary Hull, 1976

Melissa Painting in the Hallway of the Brooklyn Museum, 1978

ATMOSPHERES— WHERE TO LIVE, EAT, PAINT

Beyond the Canvas

Like all sensitives I am strongly affected by my atmosphere. I've always needed quiet, and that was sometimes a challenge in the household during my early and adolescent years. I stayed in my room or turned to nature when the going got rough.

Often nature and painting go together for me. Nature is the ultimate expression of the Feminine. She is nurturing, she can reproduce, she brings us great beauty, she supports all life. I've observed how so many of us take strength from our connection to Mother Earth. Growing up in a rural Virginia environment set the precedent for my need to recharge in the out of doors. I felt claustrophobic during the years I lived in Manhattan, without the sights and smells of the natural world. These days, weather permitting, I pack up my paints, a bottle of water with a bite to eat, and wander off wherever I can find the ingredients I need to create my painting. How the light falls is the primary ingredient, and secondary are color and my emotional feel for a scene. Finding places that have all those elements continue to be a profound experience every time…I never grow tired of it.

Melissa at the 21st Street Manhattan Studio, 1988

When I am painting on site I lose track of time and space and merge with my surroundings. Once merged, I can let go and become one with what I am painting—it's a magical experience. I enjoy experiencing the sounds and smells in nature while I work. In nature, I don't listen to music like I do when in the studio.

The preparations and schlepping for work outside mean that I need to feel physically strong to even consider it. On days when I may not have as much energy I use my watercolors, which are more portable. I have a couple of friends I occasionally go on paint-outs with that add yet another dimension, companionship, to the experience. It's a great thing, at least for this Libra gal, to have all the elements of a great situation and then be able to share it; this is the ultimate painting adventure for me. Some of these times have been among the most joyful in my life thus far.

As far as restaurants go my first question when deciding on where to eat is "what's the atmosphere like?" Living in Paris quenched my ever-present thirst for beauty. Lace curtains on the windows of traditional bistros and cafes seduced me into wandering the streets of the 18th arrondissement in Montmartre in search of something to bring home to the States. I wanted to ensure that I had the tools to transport my psyche back to memories of days traipsing through the cobblestone streets with goat cheese and baguette in hand. My Paris *atelier* (studio) had bars on the windows, and because this was part of my living space, I included them in my paintings in ways that reflected the various moods of those days.

Being hyper-sensitive to my environment means that it must be peaceful as well as quiet. In my living spaces I create the environments that I need to an extent; however, most of my creativity is reserved for my paintings. I immensely enjoyed creating dramatic atmospheres for my life-size portraits when I was painting them. It meant asking my models to bring the *accoutrements* that best described them or parts of them that I thematically wanted to emphasize. Atmosphere also included setting up the lighting just so, to further address the mood, choosing the time of day that best suited the theme and so on.

In the early days I didn't care where I had to set up my painting space. If I didn't have a studio, I set up my workspace in a hallway—wherever I could fit myself, the sitter and a large canvas. In a Brooklyn museum I was photographed in such a situation (see page 40); the museum thought the scene was so amusing that they used it on their catalog cover.

Out in the Field

"When I am painting on site I lose track of time and space and merge with Mother Earth. Once merged, I can let go and become one with what I am painting—it's a magical experience."

2011, Oil on Canvas, 16" x 20"

Kassoundra Gemini

"I have always been a fast walker,
and I flew through the streets
like a witch on a broomstick,
always the jaywalker,
daring life to slow me down."

Madame Lola, c. 1982, Oil on Canvas, 38" x 38"

NYC — LIFE IN A FASTER LANE

A brilliant man, my fellow Gary was also extremely sensitive and had discovered his ability for mediumship. Since he was always high when he stepped aside in trance, the souls that he connected with were not very evolved beings. When in a trance state he was basically absent, and I was left to acquaint myself with the personalities that visited, using his body while he was elsewhere in space and time. Although fascinating, these episodes were also scary. I attempted to learn about connecting to the other side in a safer way. Intrigued, I threw myself into reading anything on the metaphysical realms, which in those days was not much. There was no such thing as "a new age" store. There were a couple of occult shops in New York City where I was living at the time, and I boarded the subway car home with arms full of books by theosophers such as Annie Besant and Charles Webster Leadbeater. Guided by these masters, I wrapped my mind around the concept of thought-forms and Spirit Guides.

Gary and I were each awarded Max Beckmann scholarships to study painting at the Brooklyn Museum of Art. The mugging in Richmond a couple of years prior made me hesitant to move to the Big Apple, which terrified me as much as attracted me. Visions of walking through places I had heard of in Joni Mitchell songs such as Washington Square Park and Greenwich Village won out over my fears and life in New York City became my reality. Though we initially landed in Brooklyn, we soon ended up living in a tiny run-down tenement building in Chelsea that was nothing like the trendy hot spot it is today. In those days the neighborhood was largely Puerto Rican, and one woke up and fell asleep to the endless salsa rhythms loudly playing on the streets below along with sounds from the winners or losers playing on-going card games on the stoops.

Life in "the city" was beyond exciting. Looking back, I wonder if I developed an addiction then to the adrenaline rush of visiting exotic foreign places or if it is simply in my DNA. My sensitivities kept me from relaxing into my environment. In New York I had a sense of always being on edge. Gary was a punk rock fan, which meant we spent nights in the smoke-filled infamous CBGB among other more underground musical haunts. Being surrounded by the anger of the punk movement was difficult for me; I was not part of it but an observer. Days were easier; brunches at the White Horse Tavern on weekends, and even weekdays one could find me lunching leisurely in some village coffee shop with friends, discussing difficult customers from previous nights' waitress shifts before dashing off to my studio to paint before work.

Being a day person, I chose waitressing at night as a means of support since that meant I could use my best energy during the day to paint. I woefully put the brushes aside to go into work around 5 pm. In early years the shifts would most often end with drinks with workers and a blurry cab ride home in the quiet empty streets of what was then the world's busiest and most economically prosperous city. I loved waiting tables with the older gambling addicts who were my co-workers, waiting on the hookers at 4 am. At the end of my shift, I walked home through Times Square with my new black belt Aikido boyfriend Miles (Gary and I were off) feeling immune to any and all dangers. I was part

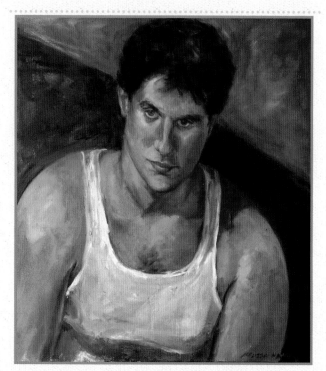

Miles Meyrow, 1987, Oil on Canvas, 16" x 20"
Photo Study *Miles Meyrow* (below)

of it all. I was still sensitive and could feel the dark energies surrounding me, but somehow I was protected. I was alive in another universe, away from the shacks in the backwoods of Virginia where I drank and made out with good-looking guys that would never see another state in their entire lives.

Deborah Dorfman, 1984, Oil on Canvas, 30" x 46"

Bob, 1976, Oil on Canvas, 62" x 76"

FIGURE PAINTING — OUT FOR EVERYONE BUT ME

During that time, anyone who came across my path was subject to being asked to sit still silently while I had my way with them in paint. I was fascinated by the exposure to different types of people, different cultures, skin colors, accents. This was all so different from the small-town atmosphere I was raised in, and I thrived on it. I have always been a fast walker, and I flew through the streets like a witch on a broomstick, always the jaywalker, daring life to slow me down. Being a child of the 60s, drugs came and went during these years. Fortunately I am not an addictive personality (save for dark chocolate) but I experienced my share of alternate realities during those years. Many people surrounding me were indeed addicted to one substance or another. The fabric of the extremes in their personalities made for scrumptious subject matter on the life-size canvases I built by myself on living room floors that served as my studios at this time. In those days one painted large. Abstract expressionism was in, figure painting was not, but that is what called to me.

Isabel's Desire, CREATRIX Publishing Line,
1984, Oil on Canvas, 68" x 76"

TEACHING & LEARNING
Beyond the Canvas

Since 1990 I've taught workshops privately and at spiritual centers such as Omega and the New York Open Center. I love to teach. It's one of the more fulfilling things I do; I get a lot from supporting and nurturing the creative spark in others. My primary focus in these classes is to help students access what they need to express and to find their own unique language in which to do so.

There are other reasons why folks appreciate my classes. Many have been damaged by criticism delivered in a less than kind way in a traditional art class. In my classes I invoke Source, or Spirit or God, Goddess (however you want to define the sacred) and I am able to hold that space for the class while students create. In this safe and sacred space they are able to delve deep inside and hear or see what abides there. Here they can let go of their fears and be free to express whatever may come up. We also use music, meditation, guided visualization and sometimes even Shamanic journey techniques to connect with our inner selves and create from that vista. I prefer to keep my classes small and intimate so that I can give a lot of individual attention.

I don't have an attachment to having folks paint like myself; in fact I encourage them to study with as many teachers as they can. Because I have a lot of formal training (including a BFA and an MFA both in Painting) I'm also available to teach them techniques. What makes my classes different is that I bridge traditional art with spiritual practices.

I ask my students to examine their intentions around the study of painting. The life of a painter is a solitary and all-consuming occupation. I know more people that have abandoned their desires to paint than those that have continued down a lonely path, that is by nature, filled with rejection; rejection from shows, grants, residencies and galleries. Artists need strong egos to handle the excitement about participating in any of the above only to be told no by those deemed to be the experts. You load your brush up with paint and keep going.

I took leave of the traditional art world long ago and carved my own way. I chose not to dwell in a world where I would be pigeon-holed into maintaining one format, style or subject matter in order to find a gallery. I never was one to brown-nose. The New York art scene, back in the day, was one that I couldn't force myself to become a part of. These days when an appropriate gallery wants to show some of my pieces, I am happy to place

Last Days of Autumn, 2008, Watercolor, 20" x 16"

them there, but I continue to maintain my autonomy and the possible need to work within more than one body of work at a time.

Do I take all that into consideration during the execution of a piece? I never did until I launched my publishing business, CREATRIX. I wasn't used to having an audience. Now, I must admit, the viewer occasionally enters my mind, but I don't allow this to influence the direction of a piece. I've had gallery owners tell me that I must consider saleability, but I need to be loyal to my inspiration and vision. If a painting finds a home, then so be it, but I can't compromise what called me to do a painting in order to be assured that it will sell. When I was doing amazing, powerful, large, expressive portraits from life, I was told over and over that my work was too personal. In my mind I was thinking how wonderful that was as I courteously exited the gallery while also feeling the pain of rejection. I'm *glad* my work is personal, no matter the price. It's also the strength of the art.

People are drawn to my loose expressive painting style. Some assume that to study painting with me would mean that they could easily learn to create paintings with that look. What they may not realize is that I have had years upon years of study in traditional technique to achieve a style that flows and appears so easy. So, do I think people need to study to be considered true artists? No, there is some great "outsider art" around, but I do find that more times than not some good formal training serves to strengthen representational art.

Fleeting Moment

"I took leave of the traditional art world long ago and carved my own way. I chose not to dwell in a world where I would be pigeon-holed into maintaining one format, style or subject matter in order to find a gallery."

2010, Oil on Canvas, 18" x 24"

For Always

" I painted all of my men and I don't regret any
time spent with them."

For Always, 2011, Oil on Canvas, 22" x 26"

Nomadic Whispers and Volatile Relationships

Whispers from the nomad inside me summoned me to go on my first visit to Europe. Significant-other Gary was back in my life, and true to his earth sign nature didn't want to go, but I bought my ticket and he followed me. We argued and drank our way through about five countries in a month-long period. He is nocturnal and I am a day person. On a typical day I'd get up early for a morning museum expedition while he slept in, hung over from the previous night's selection of phenomenal French, Italian and Spanish wines.

Back in Manhattan, we struggled to maintain our relationship, which would prove to be an on again/off again one for fourteen years. We tried to make our incompatibilities work. I admired the work of the painter Alice Neel, and Gary and I ended up unhappily recreating a scenario where one of her lovers slashed many of her canvases while in a rage. In the midst of a heated battle my own beloved Gary ripped up a favorite nude I had done of him, and I realized we couldn't go on.

There were various other men during the New York years: One was a struggling actor I met while studying the French language at Alliance Française. Though I was eager for another European foray, my actor was interested in a domestic cross-country trek, so off we went in my small Datsun pickup. I was unprepared for the fact that if you don't know someone well before you travel with them, you surely will after a few days on the road. And we were very much "on the road," having made the choice to sleep either in a tent or in the

Melissa's Pencil Drawing of Gary (torn during a fight between them), c. 1980

Let Me Love You, CREATRIX Publishing Line,
1996, Oil on Canvas, 41" x 61"

back of my truck. With nearly every stop, out came my pastels (the chosen medium for this voyage) as I attempted to capture our current destination with their chalky colors. Since my journey in this life involves learning about relationship I had successfully paired up with another "teacher" so that I could continue my process of learning about who I am and how to relate with another. The stress of the road combined with our basic differences in needs left us with no other choice than to call it quits upon our return.

There have been numerous other "learning opportunities" for me over the past many years. I painted all of my men and I don't regret any time spent with them. Being born with four planets in Libra in the seventh and eighth house of my astrological chart means that relationship is the primary arena for my soul lessons in this lifetime. Part of making lemons out of lemonade for me resulted in some of my favorite paintings. In fact most of the series I refer to as my Intimacy Series was based on me working through various aspects of a two-year relationship with Peter. I painted out the highs and lows using my brushes to help me through the rough spots.

Connect... ...ublishing Line,
16"

WHY WOMEN
Beyond the Canvas

I am often asked why I only paint women. True, if there is a figure in most of my *later* work it is a woman; however, this was not always the case. In my college years when I painted mostly life-size portraits, and even before college when I wanted to get to know someone or if I just needed a subject, my paintings included men—my fellow students, lovers or art school models. Only after I established my commercial company CREATRIX, did I transition into mainly women subjects.

The series in my greeting card line include Women and Magic, Women and Nature, Women and Dreams and so on. From a business standpoint, the decision to focus on images with women was a practical decision that would keep the line cohesive and easy to market because women buy and send more greeting cards. I could have created a series for men, but I believed that the paintings of women were easier for me to do because they have been an out-picturing of what is going on inside of me.

Looking back at my work, over the years I can see when I was painting out my loneliness, or exploring my sexuality, or celebrating my spiritual awakening. In my paintings I expressed my pain, my love of nature and my own desire for physical beauty. It's all there cloaked in the bodies of other women. Sometimes I knew why I wanted to paint someone, and many times I didn't know why I was attracted to them. Sometimes it was as simple as an acknowledgement of a beautiful head of hair or body type or a certain mystery about them. I had an unconscious desire to study aspects of myself that I either did not realize existed or could not see. We all embody various archetypes. In my conscious mind I sometimes categorized them by Goddess, Greek, or Hindu, or by Native American myths or otherwise. Everything exists in the stewpot for each of us with varying amounts of ingredients. Finally though, women are beautiful and more sensual to paint with their curves and hair.

I could state here the numerous components in my astrological chart that confirm that part of my soul's task in this lifetime focuses on the feminine, but for those of you that may not know astrology, I'll quote what my good friend and astrologer Barbara Pearl Fudala has to say:

"You have a discerning intuition or guidance system that can express itself as unusually high insight into others (psychic abilities). What this all boils down to, for me, is that you function best and are of most service to the world supporting a vision of the beauty and spirituality of the feminine which in turn supports healing and Unity for Humanity. Women (especially!) and men are uplifted by your creations and feel drawn to their journey of the Divine Feminine that you beautifully express in your art."

Aphrodite, 1995, Oil on Canvas, 48" x 66"

I value the close relationships I have with my female friends. I can't imagine my life without these deep friendships. Like the cliché goes, they are there for me in the best and worst of times. I am part of a women's group that meets once a month for sharing and support. We've been meeting for 17 years! Many of my female friends are artists, writers or musicians and/or on a spiritual path of their own, and some of them have found their way into my paintings in one way or another. I feel that my work is somehow richer simply from their presence in my life.

Melissa Painting Rhianna Mirabello for *Openings*, c. 2007, Photo by Kent Robison

I was involved intimately with another woman for a few years. Lorah is a brilliant guitarist and composer. I see sexuality as a sort of wheel, whereby one may be heterosexual or homosexual but can occasionally feel attractions that are outside of their normal sphere. My own inherent sexuality is heterosexual and there was not enough of an attraction to sustain a relationship as much as I loved my partner.

Melissa with Lorah Yaccarino, 1991

I am grateful to have had the experience not only for the love that we shared (we are still closest of friends) but because it was yet another piece for me in regards to knowing the nature of woman. There was an ease in relating that I had not experienced with men perhaps because most of the time women tend to be better communicators, and more in touch with our emotions.

I see the female body as the source of life for all of us on the planet; the Goddess is inseparable from our being, not a distant Goddess that we worship. We know this power, the ability to beget life—we know it's sacred—we know it's absolutely rooted in physicality, sensuality and sexuality. If we separate ourselves from these elements, we separate ourselves from our power. This feminine power is at the root of much of my inspiration as an artist.

Lorah Yaccarino playing Guitar (top), 1992, Photo by Melissa

Lorah Yaccarino with Guitar, 1989, Oil on Paper, 22" x 30"

Purity of Winter

"Looking back at my work, over the years I can see when I was painting out my loneliness, or exploring my sexuality, or celebrating my spiritual awakening. In my paintings I expressed my pain, my love of nature and my own desire for physical beauty."

2009, Oil on Canvas, 18" x 24"

The Seer

"Visionaries throughout time have used scrying as a means of stilling the mind to wait for answers to appear."

The Seer, CREATRIX Publishing Line,
1992, Oil on Canvas, 32" x 42"

POLAROIDS AND CRYSTAL BALLS

I have created problems for myself when I have not listened to my inner voice; however in my painting, I almost always do. There was an instructor at one of the many schools I studied who thought that everyone should see and paint like Phillip Guston. In that class we were to set up our own individual still lives and paint. As the semester went on everyone's drawings not only looked exactly alike, but looked just like the big scribbles at the nucleus of Guston's late works. I thought I was missing something and asked my classmates if that is what they really saw. They insisted they did and I wondered if I was the one going mad. I refused to paint something I did not see and instead incorporated Guston's idea that peripheral vision is important to the way one views the world.

The mediumship sessions with my painter boyfriend Gary fascinated me and I was determined to personally acquaint myself with entities on the other side. I read about spirit guides and was determined to connect with my own guides. I set up altars in the tiny purple painted living room of my dingy tenement. Affirming my fascination with the esoteric realm, a group of friends pooled resources for a very large crystal ball, one of my all-time favorite gifts. Visionaries throughout time have used scrying as a means of stilling the mind to wait for answers to appear. I note the similarity between scrying and the emptiness of a blank white canvas waiting to be defined.

It was also in this humble violet room with its ancient mantle and ornate crumbling molding that I prayed to connect with my spirit guides. I had read that all one had to do was to ask—so ask I did. I joined that invitation with my daily meditation. I met a woman at my waitress job who became a mentor to me, and after work I followed her home to her Soho loft and paid her $15 a session to teach me astrology and meditation. She subscribed to the Zen school of meditation, and my sessions in stillness today tend to follow the basic Zen protocol I learned from her.

This friend referred me to a visit with a psy-

Melissa Meditating, 1986, Photo by Edouard Boubat

chic after a frightening work-related incident. I had a difficult time with one of my bosses and disliked him. One night I dreamt that he had three heart attacks and then died. The next day I went into work and one of my fellow waitresses who shared my dislike for him informed me that he had had a heart attack the night before and was in the hospital in critical condition. I was concerned that my dislike of him followed by my dream had somehow caused his heart attack. The visit to the psychic was comforting. She explained to me that I am clairvoyant—finally I had an explanation. She discussed more on the character of my abilities, which proved helpful to me in learning how to develop my natural gifts. She also taught me how to bless my enemies, a concept that took some time for me to wrap my mind around.

I maintained a studio a couple of blocks away—a habitat that few people would be willing to deal with. Me with my dozens of six- and seven-foot canvases took up the entire basement area of another run-down tenement. There were no windows, no bathroom, and very low ceilings with plumbing pipes running close to my head and I'm short! I used to pee in a plastic bucket and sneak out after dark when the street was empty to dump it out into the gutter. I took my brushes home to wash in the tiny kitchen sink that I washed my dishes in. I did what I had to do to paint. The building was ancient and so small that one could quickly wander the eight tiny rooms crammed with canvases, paints, easels, and piles and piles of drawings. The only security was a padlock on the outside of the building to get in, but I wasn't worried since there was no reason for anyone to suspect that there was anything of value in there. I maintained that space for about seven years because one couldn't touch that amount of square footage for the $135 per month rent I paid. The landlord never raised the rent, not out of generosity (it was Manhattan after all) but perhaps out of shame.

As spirituality became more of my focus and lifestyle, the exciting nights filled with the promise of the unknown were replaced with sober conversations with the cabbies as we headed directly home. Night shifts were something to be gotten through while constantly pulling Polaroid photos of paintings in progress out of my center apron pocket to remind me of my art.

THE SPACES IN BETWEEN— MY COMFORT ZONE

Beyond the Canvas

In my college years I had always considered myself very "yang" because I was able to initiate and take action; however, a therapist pointed out to me that actually I am extremely "yin." This is because I am able to clear my mind and be receptive to what needs to arise or what I choose to allow to arise, including the information I channel when I am doing readings or Spirit Essence Portraits. This state is the same quiet state that we are in before sleep or upon waking.

I have a friend who was a midwife for years. She is currently focused on where the soul abides in between incarnations especially just before taking on a physical body. The spaces in between also fascinate me, this space is fodder for any and all possibilities. Here is the pause from life where we can learn just about anything. There are endless schools of meditation and books on this subject. In my observations, those that are willing to spend time in the still point have an advantage. Advantage over what, you ask? In my travels and reading the primary question that folks ask is "I want to know what I am here to do." In order to know the answer to that (and most other questions), I believe that it is necessary to be aware in any given moment of where our attention lies. Meditation, or going to the still point, is the most direct route.

For many the still point can be a scary place, and they will do anything to avoid it. We all have our demons. I've always needed a great deal of quiet in order to be able to hear myself think. I am fortunate that in this lifetime that I have been able to withstand the pains that have surfaced and have at times used my painting as an outlet to express my pain. This could be a literal illustration of how I am feeling or maybe an emotionally charged narrative painting. It's helpful for me to process in this way. I haven't had as many painter friends as one might think; however, the ones I've had the closest connection to are also very intuitive and share the same need for a good amount of silence. After twenty-some years I still feel connected to Kathy Burke, a painter I met back in the Paris days. After twenty-some years I still feel connected to Kathy Burke, a painter I met back in the Paris days. In the years before email, we wrote long letters filled with drawings in the margins and mailed them back and forth over the Atlantic the old-fashioned way.

Breaking Out

*"I am fortunate that in this lifetime that I have
been able to withstand the pains that have surfaced
and have at times used my painting
as an outlet to express my pain."*

1995, Oil on Paper, 23" x 29"

5 Planets in Scorpio

*"Every portrait
that is painted with feeling
is a portrait of the artist,
not of the sitter."*
~ Oscar Wilde

5 Planets in Scorpio, 1983, Oil on Canvas, 68" x 76"

PORTRAIT PAINTING

Doorways Into Souls

I was on fire, the paintings came fast and easily. *Be careful if you cross my path, I will pull you in and paint you.* There was always music from some portable boom box to carry us through the session. If it would help the sitter to be quiet and still to have a drink or smoke some pot, so be it, whatever it took to tend to my own addiction—the need to capture someone on canvas. I would usually partake of what my model was imbibing in so I could share their psychic space. I needed a muse. I needed to have the experience of surrendering myself to the unknown and visiting a foreign country by entering another's very SOUL.

The hour-long bus and subway commutes to do graduate work in painting at Queens College passed quickly since I used the commute time to study astrology. My graduate professors were not impressed by my efforts to incorporate my fascination with the metaphysical into my art, even through my efforts at defense vis-a-vis William Blake. In their defense at that time, the paintings were corny, filled with glitter and attempts at giving a visual to some of the powerful experiences I was having in my meditations. Art galleries and dealers command that an artist's work be recognizable as being done by the same person. The arguments and insistence on my part of staying true to my desire to illustrate and incorporate these events resulted in the graduate committee placing me on probation. There was only one woman on the faculty at Queens College, and she had dabbled in astrology and understood my longings but advised me to do what I had to do in order to graduate. So I did what I knew I could do well, the large, life-size portraits. The graduate committee took full credit, declaring that they had helped me find my forte, and I gracefully allowed them their satisfaction while practicing my occult studies behind closed doors. I returned to working with literal translations of my explorations into other realms some years later. I

Fallen Angel, 1984, Oil on Canvas, 48" x 66"
Photo Study of Melissa's Boyfriend Henry

Renee LeClerc with Her Painting *Emergence*, 1992

think back fondly to an image of a fellow student in the Barbara Brennan school sitting nude, her hands drawing power from a huge crystal.

I took a break from painting life-size portraits because I was more intrigued by explorations into new formats, but I acquiesced so that I might obtain my MFA. The execution of these life-size works demanded the familiar, immediate intimacy of my one-on-one sessions resulting in the emotional power and honesty that these works carry. I was Rembrandt, Spielberg and Edgar Cayce all in one. Although my self-esteem left much to be desired at this point in my life, during these sessions I was in control. I directed the sessions. I told the subject what to wear, how to sit, when they could speak. I was Queen for a Day. This was a role I knew how to play out.

In these sessions I had the opportunity to get to know someone intimately without conversation. When they looked me in the eye, *I got it*. I was so psychically tuned in to my models that I knew everything that was going on for them, where they had been and at times where they were going. I had a knack, or maybe you could call it an attraction, to catching my subjects in the midst of an emotional segment in their lives. I painted folks during a divorce, after a death, upon falling in love and right before giving birth. And I was attracted to intense personalities as well. I still am...

Spinal problems began for me with the mugging in Richmond. Massage helped, and during a massage at my local 23rd St YMCA, I experienced an awakening that I usually refer to as a "channel opening." One may also call it a Shakti opening. My life has not been the same since. When the masseuse was around my throat chakra (energy center) I felt a feeling that I can only describe as pure love. It was absolutely profound, something I had never experienced before. After the session ended I sat up in amazement only to discover that the masseuse had experienced something similar during the hour working on my body. She felt a "sweetness" around my third eye or forehead and said it was unlike anything she had experienced either. We each left the session with a feeling of awe and gratitude.

Kristen and Paul Herman with Their Painting *The Palm Reader*, 1985

Melissa with *Anything Is Possible*,
CREATRIX Publishing Line, 1986, Oil on Canvas

IN THE EYE OF THE BEHOLDER
Beyond the Canvas

A class on Aesthetics at Syracuse University introduced me to a question that continues to fascinate me: Why is a thing, person, place, beautiful to one person or group of persons and not another?

The Maori culture may not find a tall thin blonde Scandinavian woman attractive at all, while much of the Western world models itself on this as an ideal for beauty. Both beauty and art are subjective. The paintings that I prefer (in my own body of work) are not usually the more popular pieces. I enjoy witnessing what folks are drawn to when they visit my studio. I sometimes hang on to a painting for years until it eventually finds its owner, while others sell before they are finished with folks squabbling over who will purchase it. Some of the images just have the magic, the *je ne sais quoi*. And I know in the midst of creating a piece when that magic is occurring. I can't always hold onto the magic. Sometimes it floats away. If I don't keep stepping back constantly while painting, I run the risk of missing the mystery. While doing one of my Spirit Portraits, a rabbit appeared in the shape of the still to be applied paint. I stopped in awe, realizing that rabbit medicine was just what that client needed.

The popularity of one of my paintings is interesting to me. This painting was not one of my more profound artistic experiences. Because I understand how important energy is, I wonder if it is the choice of subject matter that makes this piece popular or the peaceful energy that I carried while I was creating it?

The amount of time I work on a painting varies. Therefore the events in my life can change significantly during the course of a painting. So could I conclude that a painting may have more power when the artist remains consistently in the same energetic mode or state of mind until it's complete? I suspect that is the case. And for me, the older, larger pieces that I did in one or two long sittings carry a particular power, both from the energy of my body making large strokes on the canvas as well as the fact that the sitter and I were together in one long uninterrupted session, even though there were often 12–24 hours or so in between our sessions.

I might put a piece aside for a few years, pull it out by chance to rearrange a storage rack and then see a way to make it stronger, so I dive back in and the result could be an entirely different visual or psychological statement than what I started out with.

Wicked Enchantress

*"And for me, the older, larger pieces that I did in one
or two long sittings carry a particular power, both
from the energy of my body making large strokes
on the canvas as well as the fact that the sitter and
I were together in one long uninterrupted session,
even though there were often 12-24 hours or so in
between our sessions."*

1986, Oil on Canvas, 48" x 60"

Adventure

*"After stumbling around lost in the
aromatic yellow gorse, I was found by the
facilitator, who took one look at my spaced-
out condition and instructed me to begin
weeding in the gardens in order to ground
myself."*

Adventure, CREATRIX Publishing Line,
1995, Oil on Canvas, 42" x 50"

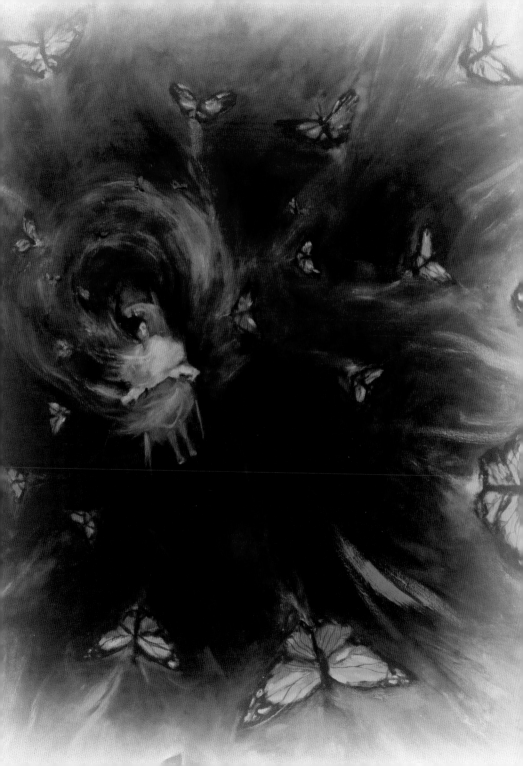

LIFE IN FRANCE
Speaking in Tongues

Through my waitressing job, I connected with a group of women who were practicing what they called *channeling*. Just as I began to experiment with my newfound group of friends, I received a prestigious Fulbright grant to study painting in Paris. As departure time grew close, Spirit intervened by magically providing me with a place to land and a mentor to help me with my less than adequate French so that I could complete the huge amount of necessary paperwork. To apply for the grant I was supposed to be affiliated with a university or someone in particular to study with, as well as being proficient in the language of the country requested to study in, neither of which I had.

My friend, translator and mentor, Ursule Molinaro, was a French citizen, and talented painter and writer. I think back with yearning (she has since crossed over) for one of our decadent afternoons filled with Ursule's wit, her black fingernails and sunglasses (she didn't allow many people to see her eyes) and of course the ever-present Gauloise cigarettes and glass or glasses of white wine. Ursule shared my interest in the occult, and we jointly attended Zoltan Mason's astrology classes once a week on the upper east side of Manhattan. Divine intervention occurred once again in the form of a customer I was waiting on during a short stint at a Rockefeller center coffee shop. His generous invitation to pick me up from the Paris airport and share his home with himself and his wife afforded me an easy arrival in the city of lights.

The section of Paris in the 14th arrondissement houses a wonderful community of dormitories for students of all nations. I was lucky to land an artist's duplex in the Fondation des Etats-Unis. Never mind there was no ventilation for the solvents and pigments I use as an oil painter; the soundproof rooms for composers and the duplexes for artists allowed me access to those who would let me practice my newfound abilities to channel. Through feedback from those I worked on I learned that I was speaking in other languages during the sessions. I have not done that since I returned from

Melissa Harris in Her Paris Studio,
1986, Photo by Edouard Boubat

France. Once I was speaking in German, a language completely foreign to me. I asked my friend to ask me when I was in trance what they were saying, and they told her to tell me to listen to *The Magic Flute*, which is a German opera.

I began to be instructed to both make sounds (now called "toning") as well as to place my hands over parts of people's bodies. I was surprised by

Portrait of Melissa Harris by David Loeb, 1985

this, but knew it was significant. I questioned what I was receiving and felt a need to study with someone skilled in those areas so that I would be in integrity in my work. Again, this was before our current era filled with sound healers and books filled with information on the subject. This sense of responsibility to those I worked with led to my decision to attend Barbara Brennan's hands-on healing school later on.

The Fulbright committee would have been surprised to learn how I was spending my time. Shortly after having an exhibition of my paintings at the American Embassy in Paris, I received a phone call from a friend who had been hired to do the wardrobe on a very high-end porno film. "Wardrobe?" you may wonder in regards to a porn film. Well, one needs lingerie, garter belts and such. She telephoned to ask if I was available to work as an extra. "No way" I replied, shaking my head as I walked back to the easel, but the phone rang again with her pleading with me to listen as she promised that I would be fully clothed in the party scene and that all I had to do was to laugh and drink champagne. *That* I could handle. *And* it would be interesting.

I worked on the film for three days. I was allowed to witness other scenes that were filmed, and fascinated, I interviewed the "actors" when they were off camera. I wanted to understand where they were coming from. I ended up giving them all readings and from there I learned more about why some of them had chosen to make a living in that way. When I returned to the USA I ventured nonchalantly into the porno section of my local video store looking for the actors I had met—and found them! They were the top names. I never found out the name of the film I worked on. It was a French, British and German production with the top stars in the industry. To this day, I remain curious and would love to see it.

Magical Findhorn, near Inverness, Scotland, set the precedent for many new age and spiritual communities that have popped up. Following a call to attend a Women and Earth Healing workshop, I commenced a low-budget journey that began with a ferry over the English Channel followed by a series of restless naps on overnight buses through England and on to northern Scotland. I made sure I was awake when we traveled by Loch Ness; I wanted to try to catch a glimpse of the famous monster bearing that name. Upon my arrival in Findhorn two days later, I was asked to go directly to work as my contract to be there was afforded by work-study. Exhausted, I pleaded to be able to

Ancient Memories, CREATRIX Publishing Line,
1997, Watercolor, 12" x 9"

nap. Ignoring the warning not to wander off into the heady fields of gorse, I lay my head down and drifted off. In a sort of half sleep I heard loudly and clearly a chorus of voices singing my name. I sat up to find no one there. I knew it was more than a dream but couldn't stay awake and drifted back into the fog of subconsciousness. Once again I heard sweet elf-like voices chanting my name. I knew I had been blessed with a special magical welcome to Findhorn. This community is known for Dorothy MacLean's communication with the devas (or heads) of the specific series of plant kingdoms. After stumbling around lost in the aromatic yellow gorse, I was found by the facilitator, who took one look at my spaced-out condition and instructed me to begin weeding in the gardens in order to ground myself.

A voyage around the north of Scotland with a fellow workshop participant remains a treasured experience. The mystical energy of that land way up in the Outer Hebrides was beautiful in a melancholy sort of way, like other sacred places I've been drawn to. I had by then visited Stonehenge a number of times but was not prepared for the wild majesty of the Callanish standing stones on the Isle of Lewis, in a place at that time desolate and out of the way with no other vertical visuals such as trees to interrupt the view (there are no trees in northern Scotland, just miles and miles of fields of peat and sheep). I had not packed my watercolors so I photographed what I needed to record and did a few paintings of the numerous stone circles and cairns, etc. to paint upon my return.

Detail from *Favorite Spot*, 2006, Oil on Board, 28" x 22"

CATS AND BUTTERFLIES— PAINTING WHAT I LOVE

Beyond the Canvas

Many of my paintings include cats and butterflies. Why? They are part of my life, I love them both, and I have been attracted to them for as long as I can remember.

Throughout time cats have been associated with witches and the paranormal. I cannot claim that there is any connection to those aspects with me, but I do know that I always loved cats. In my growing up years, I wasn't allowed to have one because my mother was afraid of them. I didn't let this deter me from continually trying to sneak cats into the house at night and hide them in my bedroom. I'd hope that I could manage to keep them without mother knowing.

I remember putting one cat in the basket that I used to haul my stash up into a tree I'd climb to hide in. As soon as I had my first apartment, I acquired a grey cat I named Oscar, the first of many felines to come. At present I'm holding down the fort with four, including a black cat, which are notorious sidekicks for witches. Cats have also long been associated with crazy old ladies and intuitives. I'm not sure why this association exists, but I do know the reasons that I am attracted to them. Cats for the most part, are easy to

Still Life with Cat, 2006, Oil on Canvas, 22" x 28"

be with and don't require as much energy as dogs (by the way, I also love dogs). Do I think cats are psychic? Certainly, but then most creatures are intuitive. If only we humans had the sense to listen and observe all creatures more. Cats are beautiful and sensual and subtle…I have a special affinity for subtlety in general.

I also had an early connection to butterflies. I often would set out on an expedition specifically to look for them. These creatures spoke to me of mystery and magic beginning in my early years.

I am not alone. Many people contact me to share mystical stories of butterflies. Most of the stories involve a relationship to loved ones that have passed over and communicated with them through the appearance of butterflies. I have my own wild stories as well. It never ceases to amaze me how incredibly beautiful butterflies are, which feeds my continuing desire to try and capture their beauty in paint. They are also fascinating because of the metamorphosis they undergo in their short lives and the transition they represent.

I once had a dream where I was being shown specifically how to paint butterflies using iridescent glazes which to date I have not completed to my satisfaction; however, I did create a series of butterfly paintings toward the end of a tumultuous relationship. These paintings helped me to process the loss I was experiencing.

Cozy Inside, 2006, Oil on Canvas, 22" x 28"

Graceful Changes

*In her time of transition, she sat quietly
and opened to the great mystery of the unknown.
In this place of in-between she found the clarity
and peace of mind to move forward on her journey.*

CREATRIX Publishing Line, 1995, Oil on Canvas, 54" x 66"

Reiki Healing Hands

"I think back to an image
of a fellow student in the Brennan school
sitting nude,
her hands drawing power
from a huge crystal."

Reiki Healing Hands, 1988, Oil on Canvas, 54" x 60"

HANDS-ON HEALING

Studying Energy Healing

Psychic reading and healing became a bigger part of my life. I felt a past-life resonance with Spain and took a five-week backpack tour alone to explore. The trip proved difficult but interesting. I didn't discover any particular reason why I felt that resonance but it felt right to follow the call before my return to the States.

Upon my return I lived in a spiritual community in upstate New York called the Pathwork Center, a place where one could study the 258 Pathwork lectures that were channeled by Eva Pierrakos from 1957 to 1979. The entity providing the lecture material was referred to simply as "the guide." Living in any kind of community is a huge teaching in itself, never mind the everyday tools for living that were required study as a part of the residency.

While there, Barbara Brennan, a Pathworker and hands-on healer, was suggested as a possible teacher. The Pathwork Center in Phoenicia, New York is located on what felt to me like Holy Land. The guide instructed Eva to be there because of this unique and sacred energy. My return to Manhattan to study with Brennan provoked mixed feelings. By this time I had lived many years in the cosmopolitan cities of Paris and New York. Breathing the Catskill mountain air energized me and living a lifestyle where I didn't need to expend energy "watching my back" let me relax into myself allowing for potential gateways of receptivity to incoming imagery and messages from Spirit. It was while living on this powerful land that I was called to paint one of my more popular images *Talk to the Moon*. I remember the night I painted it; I had walked back to my room after speaking prayers of gratitude in the Sanctuary on the property and needed to spill my overwhelming feelings onto paper. This is the way it is with me: when it comes, it comes and if I can't get to paper or canvas I am agitated until such time when I can seek a release.

High Priestess East, c. 1989, Oil on Canvas, 58" x 72"

Most of the paintings I did during this period were the illustrations of ventures into the other realms that I mentioned earlier. I think back to an image of a fellow student in the Brennan school sitting nude, her hands drawing power from a huge crystal. Another image that comes to mind is *High Priestess East*. I was introduced to a woman who made extraordinary jewelry using semi-precious stones and we proceeded to do a trade, a life-size portrait of her in exchange for two large necklaces, one to be used in my channeling and the other in my hands-on healing work. Upon completion, we transported the five-foot canvas to her Upper West Side Manhattan loft. When I went to visit her I noticed that she had placed a scarf over her face in the painting and when asked about it she communicated that she didn't like the way I had painted her face. She said it looked troubled. I explained gently that my portraits are an honest depiction and transmission of what I am experiencing in someone and that I don't even notice what the expression is because I am so entranced in the experience. Paradoxically, every time I wore the larger necklace that she had created I felt bad, my neck hurt (and not from the weight); it was a general feeling of unease. I used what I had learned to cleanse the necklace, I tried passing it through sage, a cleansing herb, and floating it in holy water. At my wit's end, I finally buried it for a month in the earth, the only element left other than fire and that solved the problem. It also proved to me the healing powers of our Mother Earth. After burying it, when I wore the necklace I felt at ease as well as empowered.

Dream Journal Paintings/Drawings, 1995, Watercolor or Ink, 4" x 6"

An Artist in Dreamtime
Beyond the Canvas

A ll possibilities exist in the nothingness.

I am often asked if my inspiration comes from dreams. I suspect that is because my watercolor images look ethereal or because some of my oil paintings alter perspective. My dreamtime is important to me. I believe the precious moments between waking and sleeping offer up fineries from our sub- and unconscious to be used like gold if we can only figure out where to put them to use.

I use dream journals in a way similar to the way people use ordinary journals. This journal is dedicated specifically to what I find in my dreams. Mostly I draw what I remember and I do this as soon as I wake up. I allow myself a maximum of fifteen minutes to write, draw or paint impressions from my dreamtime, and I do not allow myself to think about what I am putting down. I stay as connected as possible to my unconscious without having the analytical side of me interrupt the memories. In my journal I use whatever instruments are handy…paints, pen and ink, markers, etc…A Japanese ink-brush pen and a miniature watercolor set splay out onto my night-table ready to be picked up before morning tea…I also write on my journal paintings but the imagery is my primary focus. The self-imposed restriction I give myself of working on an image for a maximum of fifteen minutes provides me with both structure and freedom. I do my best to paint the images from a dream, but if I can't remember the dream, I'll use a color or something that connects me back into the emotions from the dream. I don't judge the paintings or sell these sketchy pictorials. This is a tool I use to keep me connected with my art, subconscious and emotions.

I once filled an entire journal when I was trying to work through the madness of a particular relationship. The small elegant purple leather-bound notebook held images that arose in the night while I tossed and turned through almost two years of restless sleep.

When I am thoroughly and enthusiastically engaged in creating a painting, I often dream about that piece after a painting session. In my dreams the colors stand out more clearly and I find myself looking at the painting that exists inside my mind, making changes and getting excited about returning to the easel. When I am particularly excited I may not be able to sleep because of the anticipation of the return to the painting. This sometimes leaves me sleep deprived so I have to fuel myself with dark chocolate or stop to take a nap.

Forest Fairies

*"I believe the precious moments between waking
and sleeping offer up fineries from our sub- and
unconscious to be used like gold if we can only
figure out where to put them to use."*

2010, Oil on Canvas, 28" x 38"

Life on the Road

*"When the call comes
the gypsy answers."*

Life on the Road, 1995, Dream Journal Drawing,
Watercolor and Ink, 4" x 6"

On the Road
The Sensitive Traveler

When the call comes the gypsy answers. Each place I've visited has added to my sense of who I am. I had been back in the States for awhile and was getting itchy for parts unknown. It's been my observation that once one has experienced the thrill of exploring other cultures and geographies, one will inevitably hear the call to do so again. After my return from living in Paris I felt that familiar itch to visit parts unknown. I applied for a residency for women artists in Cornwall, England that landed me in the last house before the ocean on the cliffs of a tiny town known as Saint Just. It was living here in Cornwall that paved the way for my learning how to use watercolor. I had not spent much time prior to this with the medium, having a true loyalty to the luscious feel of oils, but watercolors were really the only way that I could carry the paints in my knapsack to the remote locations I chose to paint.

Renting a car was not in my budget. I made the hike into town for groceries daily since it meant dragging whatever I had purchased uphill through fields of cows and chamomile and often in the frequent rains of the British Isles. I sucked in the salty smell of the crashing waves as I sat and painted either on the rocky cliffs, or at the sacred stone sites or even in the old and creaking house high up on the cliffs. I sat for hours painting at the tiny desk facing the ocean when it was raining too hard to go out to paint. I sensed the energies of those that had shared that space in their writing or other artistic endeavors as I moved about the house. I was there alone for a month. The nights when the shutters flapped hysterically as the ocean winds howled in a

Melissa, Early Signs of a Gypsy, c. 1959

deafening roar produced a certain amount of fear in me of ghostly spirits in a way that I had not felt before. Since this was not my first time in dealing with spirits I did what I have always done and continue to do; ask them to leave me alone and do the best I can to not give them any of my attention.

Melissa in Italy, 1981, Photo by Gary Hull

Discovering hidden, ancient sacred sites had much to do with my love of Cornwall. Daily I packed a large backpack and using a local guide-book sought out the most difficult sites I could find. This inevitably meant treading lightly over some farmer's land, quietly so as not to stir the cows into movement or noise. Upon finding these sites I was overcome with emotion, just to be in the presence of what had been spots of prayer and relevance for so many so long ago. I would sit for hours with my paints and always with a poncho, for the rains would come and wash the images right off my watercolor block and I would have to paint the scene all over again. I didn't care; *forget that I had just created a fabulous painting — I was here in this very sacred place, alone and able to absorb like a sponge the energies of the ancients.*

A psychically tuned-in friend came to visit and we rented a car to see the sites that we couldn't reach by walking. Earlier in my stay I was introduced to John Devereux, a native Brit, who has done extensive study and written several books on the earth mysteries. I was intrigued by his studies on brainwaves and dream experiences at many of these locations. He had monitored people's brainwaves while sleeping at the sites and had found the holy well in the tiny village of Sancreed to be one of the most intense. My friend and I spent an afternoon meditating inside the space of the well and did indeed experience profound connection to Spirit. The painting I did of my friend onsite there (*Woman at the Well*) remains one of my favorites. I love the energy in Cornwall and feel like I must have had a past life there.

My watercolors got another workout some months later that year when I received an invite to visit a woman in Bali. I always warn people that they'd better mean it when they invite me to visit because I will take them up on it. This invite came from a woman who had bought my greeting cards and wanted to meet me. At that time she was the only Westerner living out in the rice fields, and transportation meant me sitting behind her on her motorcycle through the bumpy fields of rice to our various locations. The Hindu society there dictated that there be numerous temples erected in each household to serve the deities. I sat before many of them attempting to capture both their beauty and the energies contained in these holy shrines. Crowds of people and many children

Bali Temple, 1993, Watercolor, 12" x 9"

Melissa in Morocco, 2000, Photo by Kent Robison

would always gather round me as I painted. I wasn't used to a culture whose attitudes about personal space differed from mine. I initially found this closeness offensive and annoying. If you can't beat them, join them, though, and thus I was forced to gracefully accept that in Bali they felt this was their right. And here I acquired some practice in what I would later need with audiences.

I've painted on every trip since those years including time in Greece, Malta, Italy and Morocco. Visually Morocco was my favorite. The magnificent tiled arches, the colorful pyramids of spices in the markets and the intricate weavings sent me into an aesthetic overwhelm. I was never completely relaxed when I painted there due to the unfamiliar treatment of women in their society. I was grateful to be traveling with Kent at the time as he would actually stand next to me while I sat on the ground and did a quick watercolor of what had caught my interest.

Tulum, Mexico, 1997, Watercolor, 12" x 9"

Woman Tipi Collage, 1995, Fabric, Feathers, Wood, Underwear,
Photos and Other Assorted Found Objects, 20" x 14" x 14"

INSPIRATION AND STYLE
Beyond the Canvas

Music creates a mood and is important when I am painting unless I am out of doors where my preference is to hear the sounds of the pounding surf or the birds singing in spring or the wind rustling the dry leaves in fall. It also helps me stay in a psychic space amplified by the sounds surrounding me for a given amount of time when I am working on a specific area of a painting or even for an entire painting session. Depending upon my mood, the genre varies from Janis Joplin to Miles Davis to New Age, Chill or World Beat. Whether it's the music or being in that receptive right brain space, through sound I enter places that sometimes surprise me, meaning that I can find myself in the previous night's dream or an event that occurred back in high school. What is consistent for me is the depth of the emotional experience. Some folks say that is the strength in my work, the feeling that it carries. I'd like to believe that is true.

Artists that have inspired me change from time to time. Some of them include Egon Schiele, Alice Neel, John Singer Sargent, J. W. M. Turner, Henri de Toulouse-Lautrec and Pierre Bonnard. What is consistent for me with each one of

Skull Collage, 1999, Bones, Beads, Feathers, Paint, 20" x 24"

them is the emotional impact of their work. As you may note, these artists are impressionists, expressionists or simply painters with a loose fluid style. I'm not interested in making a painting look like a photograph. I could, and I admire artists that do, but my art seeks to capture the essence of my subject in a style that allows direct transmission of my energy through the brush with as little effort and fussiness as possible. I merge with my subject and work quickly, allowing nothing to come between myself and my muse.

It's always been difficult for me to categorize my work because different themes, subjects or aspects bleed into others. In other words, sometimes I paint just butterflies and other times butterflies appear in paintings of women. Sometimes I paint landscapes, and other times my landscapes include figures. I allow myself to be led without analyzing why I am painting something at any given point in time. Professors and gallery directors have difficulty working with me because they are not able to put me into a particular category. In addition, I like to be free to work on several topics at different times if I feel the call, so I can't be confined. I may change canvases during the course of an hour because while working on one piece I receive insight into what might work in

another piece.

Because of this you can't call me a landscape painter or a portrait painter because though I am both of these and more, neither encompasses all that I do.

I've always collected things to use in the three-dimensional work that I occasionally do. I used to sew my own clothes and make small purses, so I would save all sorts of beads, ribbons and cords for those projects, but I also do collage. I tend to turn to collage when I don't have a lot of time to spend in the studio; that way, if I have something already started I can go in, glance at my stash of goodies and quickly add to the piece. Maybe it's a past-life memory stored somewhere, but I also enjoy working with feathers and other parts from critters.

My collage work once caused a stir at an art colony. I took the remains of a dead deer I found by the roadside and boiled the bones in bleach to clean them for use in a series of collages I was engaged in. The series also included skulls and skeletons I'd collected from various small animals. I hadn't expected the unpleasant smell from boiling the bones and folks in the colony were less than happy. I suppose most of the fellows at the residency could understand my creative need, but the staff has never quite looked at me the same. My Mom had passed away within the year prior to that artist residency. I had wondered how her death would find its way into my work. Looking back I feel that that particular group of collages was a means of working through my sadness and pondering mortality. The skulls represented her death, but the space I was in while browsing through my materials was joyous and soothing, allowing me the space to process her crossing.

Sunflowers, C. 1994, Oil on Paper, 30" x 22"

Summer Breezes

"I'm not interested in making a painting look like a photograph. I could, and I admire artists that do, but my art seeks to capture the essence of my subject in a style that allows direct transmission of my energy through the brush with as little effort and fussiness as possible."

2007, Oil on Canvas, 32" x 43"

Anything Is Possible

*"In opening to the
abundance of the Universe,
anything is possible!"*

Anything Is Possible, CREATRIX Publishing Line,
1998, Watercolor, 14"x 18"

MAKING A LIVING AS AN ARTIST

In 1990 I birthed CREATRIX, my publishing company. I, like just about 95% of the population, had been considering making greeting cards of my art. I felt there was a hole in the market that I would fill with art that celebrated the lives of women. The tagline I've used for years: artwork celebrating women's love of life, beauty, nature and magic. My cards were a smashing success in smaller mom-and-pop bookstores and in the late 90s in the New Age stores that popped up. I was determined to find a way to make my living doing something I loved. I had no business plan, didn't even know they existed, but Spirit led the way for me to fund my life through my art. I was not

Melissa's Stable Home with Kent Robison, 2003

always painting what I felt like painting, because having a card company meant I had to paint what would sell, but at least I was painting. People don't realize that much of what I was doing for many years was the very detailed work involved with running a business. I am fortunate to have the ability to be able to do that. I realize that many artists have difficulty with business. At times I felt like I was compromising myself because I wasn't painting what I wanted to in that very moment, but I held onto my dream of being able to be completely free to do that. Compromising without compromising is how a friend describes me and how I operate.

In terms of my original painting sales I have not been concerned while painting a piece about its saleability. Perhaps I'd be living a whole different life if I did. I've just never been willing to let go of what inspires me to defer to a subject, color, or landscape that might bring in a dollar. Well, maybe once or twice I added in a sailboat at Glenn's suggestion but that's about as far as it's gone. I know many of my works are dark or moody, but that was the truth for myself or my subject at that moment. Or can we separate the two? I may have been attracted to that subject since I was the one in a mood. I believe that the strength of my work comes from my willingness to be fully present with what presents itself at that point in time.

My 40s were a more stable period than any other in my life. Some health issues surfaced (the discovery of a thyroid problem along with heavy metals poisoning), which slowed me down for about three years. I didn't have the energy to work in oils, and since the heavy metals poisoning was I'm sure partly if not totally caused by my loyalty to that medium, I focused more on watercolor. Watercolors don't involve the use of solvents, and they take less energy to work with, at least for me because my watercolor painting surfaces tend to be smaller than the large canvases I like to paint with oils on. Conventional doctors couldn't diagnose my health problems and I spent a lot of time, energy and money just figuring out what was wrong. I was angry that I couldn't get back to the easel; it was all I could do to crawl into the office and onto the computer to run CREATRIX.

I was living with Kent, my partner of thirteen years, and the dynamics of our relationship provided the stability I needed to heal and grow my company. Kent had not been much for travel before we connected, but after my insistence on doing a good amount of globe-trotting he grew to love it. We enjoyed some precious experiences in different parts of Europe, Costa Rica (his favorite) and Morocco (my favorite). We lived in an old farmhouse on nine beautiful acres in the Catskill Mountains. It was here that Kent designed and built a beautiful studio just for me that would be any artist's dream. This studio was a zillion miles from my old bathroom-less studio in the city. It had French doors that open onto a meadow surrounded by forests, skylights, and six-foot windows with plentiful light. I had paid my dues with crappy workspaces and that along with other emotional factors made me feel so intimidated by this space that it took me about six months before I could enter the studio without bursting into tears.

Kent and I are grateful for the life we shared together; however, life eventually called us in different directions.

I know that I have to be very careful about what I ask for, because most of the time I will get it. At the top of my wish list after Kent was a request for a passionate man who liked to meditate. Glenn encouraged me to meditate more and was as passionate about being in nature and living in the moment as I am, probably more. We shared a love of the ocean and every weekend was spent in the same way. We packed what we called the "art

Melissa and Kent Robison, c. 2003

Woman Who Wanted It All, CREATRIX Publishing Line,
1991, Watercolor, 9" x 12"

cart" (a durable cart that held both my art supplies as well as a picnic) and headed off usually to Harkness Memorial State Park in coastal Connecticut. Upon arrival, I set up to paint in the lovely gardens on the 230 seaside acres. Glenn would go to scout out our spot on the beach and I joined him after my painting session. He was a positive influence in encouraging me to take more time for pleasure, something that left to my own devices I tend to neglect. These were blissful, magical days. Sadly, we were not meant to be a forever couple, our differing needs in relationship ultimately dictating that we go our separate ways.

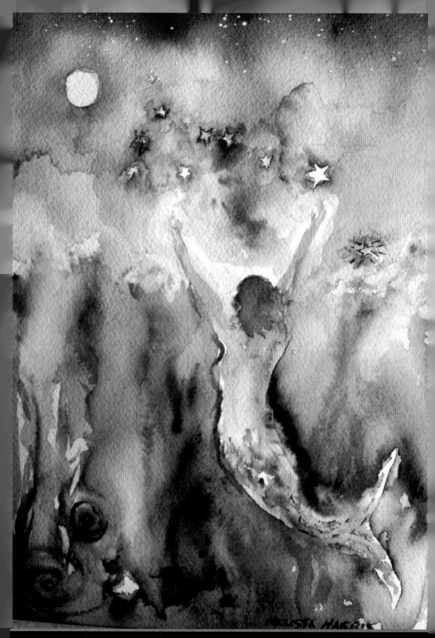

SPIRIT ESSENCE PORTRAITS AND HEALING
Beyond the Canvas

I experienced a turning point in 1988 when I was attending Barbara Brennan's hands-on energy healing school. I was working as a waitress in the evening, painting during the day and on my night off attending healing school. Back in those days the class was taught by Barbara Brennan herself to a group of twelve of us in a tiny New York office. The homework for her class was extensive and very time consuming. I was overwhelmed. Painting takes literally endless amounts of time. I felt pulled in all directions—painting, supporting myself, being a healer. I knew that I was skilled at the healing work. How could I let this go when the world needed to be saved? It was a difficult decision, but after a year of training with Barbara, I decided not to return to the Brennan school and focus solely on my art. I knew that there would come a time when I would return to esoteric studies and practice because of my deep interest in this area.

About seventeen years later I connected with a group of friends that were regularly channeling. I responded to the call I felt to reconnect with others who were doing that sort of work and somehow squeezed in a few hours (sporadically) to share channeling experiences. I had a desire

Magic Wand, c. 2008, Watercolor, 7" x 10"

to combine, in a direct way, channeling with my painting. Since I love to travel, I thought it was a good idea to offer these sessions to some special accounts that were purchasing my CREATRIX products. I would tune in psychically to an individual and then create a narrative watercolor of what I received when I tuned in, either by clairvoyance or by clairsentience (feeling what the other feels) or by hearing and *knowing*.

These sessions continue to be very well received. The process continues to change since I began doing these. Sometimes it's difficult for me to figure out what I am receiving so I have learned to tell the client everything that I am receiving. It may not make sense to me but it almost always does to them. One of my favorite examples of this process by way of its oddity is the time I kept seeing those old-fashioned scrub boards women used to use to wash clothes. I saw it about three times before I gave in and mentioned it to the client. She was not at all surprised because it turned out she collected them. Another instance was the time I repeatedly saw a white horse in relation to a woman's husband. The client wasn't surprised since that was a special symbol for her and her husband. I don't remember the entire significance but I do know that they had already determined that the white horse was special and one day while on their honeymoon they were walking on the beach speaking about it and looked down to discover a plastic white horse on the sand! The stories go on and on...

Some of my guides have a sense of humor and for a time period were giving me information by way of corny lyrics in old 50s and 60s songs. While sitting in my usual receptive mode, the words and melodies of the songs began playing in my

Painting a Doorway, c. 2008, Watercolor, 7" x 10"

head. I'd tell the client what song it was and we would laugh about the obvious meaning to them.

I love doing these sessions for a few reasons. In my "normal at-home life," I am in the studio alone all day, so the intimate one-on-one time with new people is great. Because I enjoy travel that becomes an additional bonus when I visit stores or centers to do these sessions. And finally I'm glad to be of help. I am fascinated by the common themes that arise in folks' (mainly women come for these) lives, and I am touched by the fact that what most people want to discover is how they can make a difference in our world. The question I am most often confronted with is "What am I here to do?" My desire to make art and my desire to be a healer merge here, as do my abilities in my painting classes when I help gently nudge others a step further on their own path.

One of the questions that I sometimes ask during a Spirit Portrait session is "If you could have three things that you wanted what would they be?" and the initial reply is, "Wow, I never thought about it."

I'm surprised at the number of people that think that life happens *to them* since I live by the concept that we are, *in every moment, creating our own reality.* I prove this belief to myself daily in every area of my life but sometimes I need reminders. When I meet someone who has the potential to be significant in my life a sort of "light goes on" for me. That's about the best I can do to describe it. It's a knowing. Some years ago I met a woman who offered a coaching series addressing this theme of creating your reality. I was hesitant about committing—the consultation series was pricey—but the day after I committed someone contacted me from the web and purchased a painting priced for that same amount.

The practice I learned from this coaching series necessitates being very clear about any change I want to create. Using this tool along with meditation has helped me discover what may stand in the way of what I wish to manifest and then to do what I need to move toward that change. I'm so grateful for the many creations in my life since working with this coach.

It seems that most of us have an urge to create and/or to leave a piece of ourselves behind, to make our mark. I am touched by that. I love participating in the process of watching others doing so, either by helping with their creative process or by sharing what I see for them as guidance in my readings. I have hope for the future because it feels to me as if people are waking up in exponentially growing numbers. Certainly in my own journey I continue to open to growth and change, since for me change and growth are all there is.

Thank yous go to all my friends and family that have supported me and put up with the necessity of the selfish lifestyle of an artist. Artists need amounts of alone time that are almost impossible to deal with and this means that inevitably some people along the way will be disappointed or downright angry. I do my best to maintain balance.

Go For It!

For all the times you thought
you couldn't do it,
There are 10 times as many
reasons why you can!

CREATRIX Publishing Line, 1994, Watercolor, 7" x 10"

The Tarot Reader

"Some people fall back on waitressing,
I fall back on psychic readings."

The Tarot Reader, 1986, Oil on Canvas, 76" x 70"

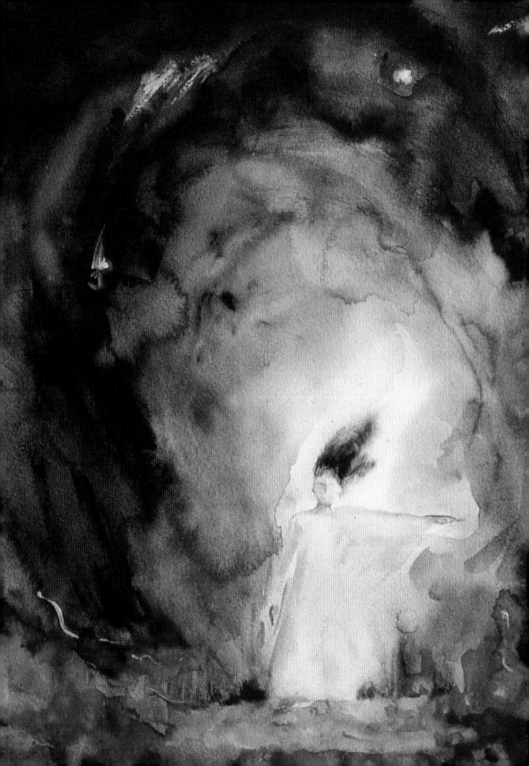

DAY JOB
Psychic Reader

When I began CREATRIX there was an independent flavor to greeting cards, and my line
sold very well to the many independent stores
that loved my work. In the mid 2000s the market
changed, and I needed to be able to compete with
larger companies. These companies printed over-
seas and offered incentives I could not compete
with such as dozens of free cards and free card
racks, etc. to a rapidly shrinking number of retail
outlets. I continue to adjust to supply my CREAT-
RIX customers with the products they have come
to love. I had stopped doing readings in the early
90s because the strong sense of responsibility I felt
to my clients was too much for me at the time. I
take the readings very seriously and am careful
to frame information in a positive way that will

Ivira DePuela, Spirit Essence Portrait, 2012

best help the client. Psychic readings will always be one of my "day jobs." The readings are a labor of love. I enjoy helping where I can and based on feedback from my clients my work serves that purpose. There is never enough time to paint. Being an artist is like carrying another whole person alongside you, and you have to be able to carry that extra person every-where, all the time.

As I look back at the archetype of the artist as struggling and having a dramatic, emotionally charged, chaotic life, I wonder if I have diverted much, if at all from the cliché. Am I unhappy with the way my life has turned out to date? Not really. Sure, there are some things I would change if I could go back and re-create. I'd love to know where I will end up living and who my next love will be but I believe if I vision it I'll create it and in the meantime it's fun to imagine. My life has been colorful and exciting, full of travel, adventure, romance and of course remarkable spiritual experiences. I could happily do without any more diversions from my painting, so I am much more judicious in my choices. I'm continually looking to find a balance between my love of adventure and the stability I need in order to maintain my work. Most likely it will always be a juggling act.

Melissa Painting Jackie Ellsworth's Portrait, 2010 Photo by Melissa Ellsworth

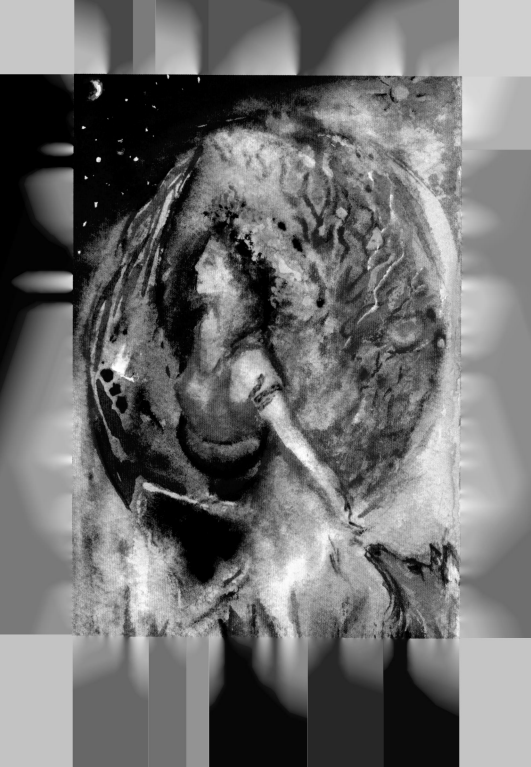

SPIRIT GUIDES
Beyond the Canvas

When I explain that I work with my Spirit Guides, I am often asked to explain more about who they are. Guides come and go depending on what we need at any given time.

In the beginning of my work with other realms of consciousness, a psychic I visited told me that one of the entities working through me was a Native American healer known as Three Black Feathers. Shortly after hearing this, two fascinating incidents validated the information I had received. I was at my chiropractor, and after the treatment he told me that while standing behind me he saw a Native American man with a blackbird. I wasn't close with him and he had no way of knowing about my guide so I was excited that he validated what the psychic had told me. Around that same period of time, I was working on a friend (a non-believer in anything esoteric) doing a hands-on healing homework session, and my friend told me that while I was standing by her midsection she saw "an American Indian guy" with a blackbird on his shoulder. Again, I had not mentioned anything to her about Three Black Feathers.

I find it difficult to describe how I actually experience entities energetically. Do I feel angels? Who is it that is speaking to me? In a session is it my guides coming through or those of the clients? Being a bottom-line person my answer is (not to be flippant)—"I don't really care." Please understand that I don't claim to be an expert on the subject of guides nor do I suggest that guides can't be experienced in a more defined way. I do discern differences in frequencies, and I occasionally may have a glimpse of a guide that chooses to appear to me in a form I can recognize. From what I have read and experienced I think that our helpers cooperate to the best of their abilities and help us to first of all trust them and then to be able to understand the information they are trying to impart. I believe that we attract different guides at different points in our lives for specific reasons. And, because at a certain turning point, due to a limited amount of time and energy for my painting, I made the conscious decision to make my art my priority and put the healing work aside, I let go of any attachment to focusing on the bearers of the information and stayed intent on simply receiving the info. All that being said, I experienced Three Black Feathers' energy as sort of "heavy, intense and low-key but serious." Other guides have felt like pure light or tinkling sparkly energy. Sometimes the energy is so strong and powerful that it's difficult to sit with. The guides find ways to communicate to me or through me and I'm grateful for their help.

Reflecting

"Other guides have felt like pure light or tinkling sparkly energy. Sometimes the energy is so strong and powerful that it's difficult to sit with."

2011, Oil on Canvas, 11" x 14"

For a Dreamer

*"There have been so many beautiful
summer days when friends are out
swimming or barbecuing or attending
concerts where I have chosen to hole
myself up in the studio of the moment
because that is the only time the model
could show up or because I began a
landscape painting the day before at that
time of the day and I must capture the
exact same light so as to continue the
painting."*

For a Dreamer, CREATRIX Publishing Line,
1992, Oil on Canvas, 66" x 68"

IS IT WORTH IT?

Sacrifice

Unlike some artists who are un- or under-appreciated until death, I've enjoyed the opportunity in my life to witness the affect my work has had on other people. I'm grateful to have received some recognition, appreciation and admiration and not posthumously. As an artist I am the mother to my paintings yet I am different from most mothers. Mothers give birth to children but the mother and child do not exist in the same form forever. Once created, artwork (my children) lives on and remains alive, willing and able to affect future generations. I wonder what definitive statement people will make about my art when I'm gone?

The question I have asked myself over and over is whether the sacrifices I have made to be a painter are worth it. I always come back to the

same thing. For me there is no other choice but to paint. On top of becoming very grumpy in a life without art—what would l be living for? —there is always the next image to capture.

Melissa Painting at Harkness Memorial State Park in Connecticut, 2009, Photo by Glenn Sloss

Melissa's Dream Studio, c. 2010

Even now, as I look out on my funky screened-in porch, I'd love to put aside this writing and capture the light as it's falling on Timmy, the old man of my fantastic bunch—the fab feline four. There have been so many beautiful summer days when friends are out swimming or barbecuing or attending concerts where I have chosen to hole myself up in the studio of the moment because that is the only time the model could show up or because I began a landscape painting the day before at that time of the day and I must capture the exact same light so as to continue the painting.

I'll never forget one of the few times I succumbed to a desire to travel with a group of friends. Most people upon visiting a new country want to sightsee, shop, eat, drink, etc. Upon landing in Santorini, Greece, Kent, my partner at the time and I, found ourselves in what we referred to as "the hovel"—our closet-sized hotel room right on the cliffs. Just as the sun was setting, the gang was off for shopping and dinner. On the stormy grey sea just below floated a beautiful steamer—the sky above was an other-worldly mix of vermillion and blue grey. It was sheer torture leaving the hovel to join the others. I scrambled to splash some watercolor on paper in those few short moments before we had to leave, and to this day I still yearn to go back to that room to capture what I am sure would be one of my more intriguing sunset paintings. The others had been having a leisurely drink in those moments before and laughing over our follies of the day, relaxing, enjoying themselves as I held court on the teeny bed alone in the hovel desperate to make this one perfect dusk in Greece my own, to put my signature on this majestic piece of landscape.

Is the sacrifice worth it? Absolutely!

In Gratitude, CREATRIX Publishing Line, 2005, Oil on Paper, 32" x 40"

Jameen Photo Study (top),
Warrioress, 1992, Oil on Canvas, 36" x 40"

ABOUT EMPOWERMENT
Beyond the Canvas

I grew up during the rise of the feminist movement, which perhaps also added to my focus on the female gender. Growing up, empowered women role models were sparse. In fact an empowered woman in the rural South was an oxymoron. I tried to select the best of the available role models. My babysitter Chestine was the quintessential beautiful willowy blonde who went on to become a flight attendant. In those days that meant that one had to be the cream of the crop in the appearance department. I wanted to be Chestine and did what I always have done, tried to suss out what made a Chestine. I worked for my father in his optometric office off and on during high school and college and was fond of his secretary with her platinum blonde hair, feminine pastel colored cardigans and manicured nails. My relationship with my mother and each of these other women fed me in some way but I could not say that any of them embodied a woman standing strong in her power; a woman that knew her strengths and used them to create her reality and inspire others.

I've worked hard to empower myself. This has included

traditional therapy, astrology, energy work, Pathwork Studies, Native American, Buddhist, and Wiccan practices and other assorted workshops and readings sprinkled in here and there. All of it was well worthwhile and contributed to a stronger, wiser, more conscious me.

Perhaps because of my early role models I enjoy doing what I can to empower those I work with. Whether it's helping them get in touch with their creativity in workshops, or revealing what I see as I tune into them psychically and thereby hopefully aiding in their path toward wholeness, it's about empowerment. I care deeply about how we, as a civilization, are disrespecting Mother Earth. I feel that by each of us standing in the truth of who we really are, we can in that way come to affect the change that is necessary to be able to bring our planet back into a balance. And *how do we stand in the truth of who we really are?* Some ways include being present in the moment, allowing our vulnerabilities, feeling our pain, expressing ourselves, and not betraying ourselves. Self-help and consciousness-raising materials are plentiful these days. Choose a path and walk it.

In Your Power

Ground and center yourself.
Call on your connection to Spirit.
You have everything you need within you.
Stand in your power.

CREATRIX Publishing Line, 2005, Watercolor, 20" x 26"

Openings, 2007, Oil on Canvas, 42" x 48"

BONUS SECTION

12 TIPS TO OPEN THE DOOR
TO YOUR PSYCHIC AND CREATIVE SELF

In my observations much of what needs to occur in our psychic and creative processes is a state of awareness. Use the tips on the following pages to fine-tune these abilities in your own practice.

PSYCHIC AWARENESS

1. Meditate on a Regular Basis.

Why? *In my experience meditation is the best tool. When we meditate we are completely present in the moment. From this still point anything can happen. Often this can include deepening our connection with the core of our being, Spirit, Spirit Guides and All That Is. We experience a sense of peace by meditating which allows all else in our life to flow with ease.*

2. Connect with Your Spirit Guides.

How? *I start by speaking to them out loud and asking for their guidance—this lets them know I want to connect. If you haven't made a connection, continue to talk to them and be aware that their response might be very subtle.*

3. Practice Your Awareness of Being in the Present Moment.

What does that mean? *Several times a day take notice of what you are experiencing through each of your senses. Also take note of where you are emotionally. Make this a habit.*

4. Make it a Practice to "Hear, Feel, See or Know" Guidance and Discern its Source.

How will I notice and how will I know where it is coming from? *This comes back to becoming more aware in any given moment. For me, when information comes from my core self or senses, I can remember it easily and there is a feeling of familiarity. When information "drops in," it could be in the form of a creature representing something meaningful for you or someone calling and* *discussing something that could be an answer to an issue you might be dwelling on — things like that.*

5. Keep a Daily Review.

What is this? *When I lived at the Pathwork Center studying the lectures of Eva Pierrakos, we had an assignment of noting at the end of every day if and where we were not at peace with an interaction. For example, you may have spoken harshly to someone and didn't apologize or perhaps someone spoke harshly to you and you didn't speak up for yourself. You would look back on the day and become aware of when you were not at peace (a gut knowing). In doing this we became more aware in the moment and would be more careful to always be kind and in the reverse, speak up when others have been unkind to us. A daily review is an exercise in awareness.*

6. Express Your Love Freely.

What does this have to do with anything? *I don't know if I can explain it well. What I know is that when I am in a state of unconditional love I am closest to Spirit, God or however you look at the Divine. In this state I do not judge. I suggest that you practice on friends and family and extend out from there and notice the shift in your life.*

CREATIVE DEVELOPMENT

7. Keep a Dream and/or Traditional Journal.

What is a dream journal and why should I do this? *I paint my dreams in a small journal or I write them down or do a combination of both. This helps me stay connected to my unconscious which I have found holds a storehouse of helpful information. For example, sometimes I discover that my psyche is still dwelling in an area that I thought was resolved; I might get a great visual for a painting. Or I may find that a dream has stirred up a memory that could be helpful in a current situation. Possibilities are endless.*

8. **Keep a Notebook and Camera on Hand to Document Ideas.**

I have a good memory so why should I do this? *I used to think that I would remember but I often don't. If you paint from life it's especially help-ful to photograph a particular tree or cloud etc., for later use in a painting. In terms of ideas—as I mentioned earlier if the source of the idea is external, it is more difficult for me to remember so I always keep a small pad of paper handy to record my thoughts.*

9. **Create Your Intentions and Take Steps toward Achieving Them.**

What if I don't know how to move forward? *Take small steps, any small movement in a day, such as a phone call to gather information or a search on the internet. This counts. We may not know how to get where we are going but if we can relax about that and allow a gentle flow, things may fall into place before we know it.*

10. **Notice What Inspires You and Put More of That in Your Life.**

How do I put more of that in my life when I am so busy? *It can be as simple as wearing a color that you love, putting music on as you begin your day, having your coffee outdoors and watching the light change. It begins with an awareness of what inspires you. For example, I am always inspired to paint when I am in a different landscape but I may be just as inspired from hearing a new song that stirs something in me.*

11. **Choose an Outlet for Your Creativity, Commit on Some Level and Show Up on a Regular Basis.**

I feel pulled in many different directions and end up doing nothing. *I can relate to this but at a certain point we have to make a choice and stick to it. And then we have to show up in order to be able to maintain our connection. If we stay away too long it becomes difficult to enter back in.*

12. **Follow Your Creative Urges!**

THE ARTIST AND THE EGO: USING REJECTION AS A CATALYST

If you want to be an artist, rejection goes along with the territory. We can apply to show our work and get rejected. We can apply for grants and artist residencies and get rejected. We can have a showing of our works and sometimes not a single painting sells. There is a job title, "art critic," and believe me there are lots of those folks in the world! Art evokes emotions and opinions. All this rejection is part of the path, the blows an artist takes in the line of duty. Rejection can't be avoided unless one creates art simply for one's own sake or pleasure.

In my observations it is a natural tendency for an artist to want to show others what we have painted, or written or choreographed. I suppose I could say it is always for approval; however, the reason for the approval may vary. Often we want approval for the content of the creation but sometimes it may just be to show ourselves that "Yay! I did it!" When we release this artistic statement into the world, people will love it, hate it or be indifferent. That release of our art can give us pleasure, but what happens to the fragile artist's ego when our precious works do not succeed or are not accepted in the ways we had hoped? Do we stop painting just because people have said mean or cruel things? Not me. I paint because I must.

I myself have had about a hundred times more rejections than acceptances. I've got a tendency, actually it is stubborn streak, which has served me well with accepting rejections. If you tell me "No" I'll work that much harder and find my own creative way around the rejection to gain success in a different form. I realize that this is not a normal tendency – it just happens to be part of my innate personality structure. To get to this place I've done a lot of personal work using various therapies to strengthen my delicate ego. I still feel that same pain upon receiving any negative response, but it doesn't last as long as it used to and before

I know it, I've moved on to the next focus. I've realized that it does no good to dwell in the negative. So I allow myself to feel the pain and then pick myself up, dust myself off and move ahead. If I allowed myself to dwell on all the times I have been rejected, it would stifle my creative process and I won't allow anything to do that. I have a talk with myself saying something like "Hey—this hurts, it makes me angry or feels unfair, but I know I'm a good artist. I believe in this creation, it may or may not be my best piece of work, perhaps I should have chosen another for this application process, but it was an incredible journey to make it. I choose to accept this, I love what I have created and I'm moving on."

In this way I am using the rejection as a catalyst. It also helps to be flexible. An artist should master the form they love and not conform. After all, we had the concept or vision to begin with and if it doesn't fit the mold or suit other people's tastes aesthetically, so be it. Move on. Create a new mold. Don't get stuck. Our art will not be pleasing to everyone. I carry the voices of two very successful artists in my head advising me to stick to my original visions when I have considered the alternatives and I replay their words when needed. There have been times when I have considered conforming but I knew that that would not be "in truth" and since being in truth is front and center of my belief system, it would not have worked for me anyway.

That being said, I've found that I have had to be *flexible* and there is a difference between flexibility and conforming. I listen well to what it is that the other requests and feel into how I can achieve that without compromising my own wants. An example that comes to mind immediately is this book cover. My designer wanted to use a photo of me on the cover; I wanted to use a painting. After days of negotiating different images, testing out both photos of me and paintings, it just was not working. My response was to march into the studio and paint the self portrait that is on the cover of the book. It worked out great! The designer got what she wanted—an image of me—I got the painting I wanted. Conversely I think back on a particular venture whereby I didn't listen to my gut and see how that decision may have affected the life of that project. Every time I look at it, I am reminded of my initial instinct and also remember partially wanting to please the person I was working with.

So to all the artists and aspiring artists, I say: Stay strong, trust your gut, and believe in yourself. The idea or image came to you so be true to your vision. Writing this book was a soul task for me, something *I* felt strongly that I needed to do, and in the manner in which I needed to write it. I was asked to write a book before but the nature of their request differed from the vision I had and it did not come to fruition. There is a magic when things just flow. It's been very fulfilling to allow the process that occurred when I set out on this project which was to open up and let things flow. I had help on the structure but the contents had a life of their own and I could not have completed it until certain events in my life had transpired. These events provided the wisdom and experience to be able to put into words the material that describes my own journey as a psychic and an artist. The book could be rejected, could be lauded…I just had to do it. I don't regret having chosen this path.

As I enter what feels like a new phase of my life in many aspects, including my art, my confidence is stronger than ever. I trust more in my decision making process whether with art or marketing or otherwise. I can't wait to dive into the next series brewing itself inside of me and discover how this new stage of life finds its way into my work.

Thank you for sharing my journey.

A Few Other Favorite Paintings

Many of my favorite paintings are featured throughout this book. I've added a few more in this section for several reasons. Some paintings are here because they are good paintings in the ways that I learned to make a "good painting" in art school. Others are here because of their emotional impact and some are here because they are close to my heart in a sentimental way.

Dreams Come True

I love this large painting not only because I think it's beautiful but because the woman in the painting (Ja-lene Clark) is my good friend and designer of this book. It was inspired by a photo I took of Ja-lene in a favorite spot in central Florida. Since then many of her dreams have come true, hence the title.

2009, Oil on Canvas, 26" x 36"

Timmy

Timmy is the oldest of my four felines. I love the peaceful feeling in this painting created partly by the way the light falls and partly by Timmy's beautiful personality—though he's more spunky than peaceful. It was a rare moment.

2006, Oil on Canvas, 24" x 18"

Transcending Cat

The simple composition in this piece lends to the power of its impact. I also like the intensity of expression on the cat's face. Jazz, the cat, has since passed on. RIP Jazz.

2006, Oil on Canvas, 24" x 24"

Evening in February

*I love the feeling that I captured here. There is
a loneliness that comes across. I remember the
conversation we were having and I felt I captured the
content of our communications in the piece.*

1993, Oil on Paper, 23" x 30"

Warm Winds

*I love remembering times I sat out in the lava fields —
very uncomfortable but loving every moment of the
marshy smells of the sea between the lava mounds, the
sounds of waves crashing and the edgy energy of the
Hilo side of the Big Island in Hawaii. This piece is not
as loose as I like my watercolors but close enough. I can
almost smell the ocean when I look at it.*

2011, Watercolor, 10" x 7"

Path by the Rocks

*Not necessarily a masterpiece but one of my early large
watercolors. The day was magical so the painting has
sentimental meaning for me.*

2011, Watercolor, 20" x 16"

Limbo

I consider a painting to be successful not because it is pretty necessarily but because I was able to transfer what I was feeling (or what the subject was feeling) in the painting. I was going through a breakup and used a photo I had taken of a particular model as the vehicle to convey my own depression.

2011, Oil on Canvas, 22" x 28"

Sapphire

This very large portrait of the author Sapphire is nice and loose and painted in the way I stylistically like the most. I also like the color scheme as well as the emotional intensity created by Sapphire's expression and heightened by the treatment of the Goddess dolls that Sapphire made.

1989, Oil on Canvas, 44" x 60"

Painting Outside the Lines Visual Art List

(Visual art is numbered in the order of appearance in the book. Art that appears in the book without captions is listed in boldface and referenced below.)

INTRODUCTION
1. Melissa at Altar During Ceremony (photo).

PSYCHIC CHILD—WHY AM I DIFFERENT?
2. *Blessing Tree,* 3. **Outside of Time**[1], 4. *Early Butterfly Art,* 5. Melissa with Mother Sally (photo), 6. Melissa in Sunhat (photo), 7. Dad Donald, Melissa, Mother Sally (photo), 8. Melissa with Mickey (photo).
BEYOND THE CANVAS: THE EMPATHIC ARTIST
9. *Invocation* Photo Study, 10. *Invocation,* 11. *Dream Angel.*

YOUNG ADULTHOOD
12. *Sing Out,* 13. **Daydreaming**[2], 14. Melissa with Her Cat Jupiter (photo), 15. Melissa with Gary Hull (photo).
BEYOND THE CANVAS: ATMOSPHERES— WHERE TO LIVE, EAT, PAINT
16. Melissa Painting in the Hallway of the Brooklyn Museum (photo), 17. Melissa at the 21st Street Manhattan Studio (photo), 18. *Out in the Field.*

NYC—LIFE IN A FASTER LANE
19. *Kassoundra Gemini,* 20. *Madame Lola,* 21. Miles Meyrow Photo Study, 22. *Miles,* 23. *Deborah Dorfman,* 24. *Bob.*
BEYOND THE CANVAS: TEACHING AND LEARNING
25. *Isabel's Desire,* 26. *Last Days of Autumn,* 27. *Fleeting Moment.*

NOMADIC WHISPERS AND VOLATILE RELATIONSHIPS
28. *For Always,* 29. **Stasis**[3], 30. Gary Torn (photo), 31. *Let Me Love You.*
BEYOND THE CANVAS: WHY WOMEN
32. *Connecting the Circles,* 33. *Aphrodite,* 34. Melissa Painting Rhianna Mirabello (photo), 35. Melissa and Lorah Yaccarino (photo), 36. Lorah Yaccarino with Guitar (photo), 37. *Lorah Yaccarino with Guitar,* 38. *Purity of Winter.*

---

1 *Outside of Time,* 2012, Oil on Canvas, 18" x 14".

2 *Daydreaming,* 1990, Oil on Paper, 14" x 20".

3 *Stasis,* 1996, Oil on Paper, 23" x 15".

POLAROIDS AND CRYSTAL BALLS
39. *The Seer,* 40. ***Spirits in the Window***[4], 41. Melissa Meditating, Photo by Edouard Boubat.

BEYOND THE CANVAS: THE SPACES IN BETWEEN— MY COMFORT ZONE
42. *A Change in Course,* 43. *Breaking Out.*

PORTRAIT PAINTING—DOORWAYS INTO SOULS
44. *5 Planets in Scorpio,* 45. ***The Alchemist Den***[5], 46. *Fallen Angel,* 47. Photo Study Henry, 48. Renee LeClerc with her Painting *Emergence* (photo), 49. Kirsten and Paul Herman with Their Painting (photo).

BEYOND THE CANVAS: EYE OF THE BEHOLDER
50. Melissa with *Anything is Possible* (photo), 51. *Wicked Enchantress.*

LIFE IN FRANCE—SPEAKING IN TONGUES
52. *Adventure,* 53. ***The Wonder of It All***[6], 54. Photo by Edouard Boubat, 55. *Portrait of Melissa Harris* by David Loeb, 56. *Ancient Memories.*

BEYOND THE CANVAS: CATS AND BUTTERFLIES— PAINTING WHAT I LOVE
57. Detail from *Favorite Spot,* 58. *Still Life with Cat,* 59. *Cozy Inside,* 60. *Graceful Changes.*

HANDS-ON HEALING—STUDYING ENERGY HEALING
61. *Reiki Healing Hands,* 62. ***Talk to the Moon***[7], 63. *High Priestess East.*

BEYOND THE CANVAS: AN ARTIST IN DREAMTIME
64. Dream Journal Paintings/ Drawings (photo), 65. *Forest Fairies.*

ON THE ROAD —THE SENSITIVE TRAVELER
66. *Life on the Road,* 67. ***Woman at the Well***[8], 68. Melissa, Early Signs of a Gypsy (photo), 69. Melissa in Italy, Photo by Gary Hull, 70. *Bali Temple,* 71. Melissa in Morocco, Photo by Kent Robison, 72. *Tulum, Mexico.*

---

4 *Spirits in the Window,* 1985, Oil on Canvas, 16" x 20".

5 *The Alchemist's Den,* 1986, Oil on Canvas, 74" x 80".

6 *Wonder of It All,* 2008, Oil on Canvas, 16" x 20".

7 *Talk to the Moon,* CREATRIX Publishing Line, 1987, Watercolor, 9" x 12".

8 *Woman in the Well,* CREATRIX Publishing Line, 1997, Watercolor, 9" x 12".

Beyond the Canvas: Inspiration and Style

73. Woman Tipi Collage (photo), 74. Skull Collage, Bones, Beads, Feathers, Paint (photo), 75. *With Soul*, 76. *Sunflowers*, 77. *Summer Breezes*.

Making a Living as an Artist

78. *Anything Is Possible*, 79. **Queen of Hearts**[9], 80. Melissa's Stable Home with Kent Robison (photo), 81. Melissa and Kent Robison (photo), 82. *The Woman Who Wanted It All.*

Beyond the Canvas: Spirit Essence Portraits and Healing

83. *Joy*, 84. *Magic Wand*, 85. *Painting a Doorway*, 86. *Go For It!*

Day Job—Psychic Reader

87. *The Tarot Reader*, 88. **Spirit Signs**[10], 89. Ivira DePuela, Spirit Essence Portrait, 90. Melissa Painting Jackie Ellsworths' Portrait, Photo by Melissa Ellsworth.

Beyond the Canvas: Spirit Guides

91. *Goddess of All Things*, 92. *Reflecting*.

Is it Worth It? —Sacrifice

93. *For a Dreamer*, 94. **Into the Light**[11], 95. **A Different Point of View**[12], 96. Melissa Painting at Harkness Memorial State Park in Connecticut, Photo by Glenn Sloss, 97. Melissa's Dream Studio (photo), 98. *In Gratitude*.

Beyond the Canvas: About Empowerment

99. Jameen Photo Study, 100. *Warrioress*, 101. *In Your Power.*

12 Tips To Open the Door To Your Psychic and Creative Self

102. *Openings*.

My Favorite Paintings

103. *Dreams Come True*, 104. *Timmy*, 105. *Transcending Cat*, 106. *Evening In February*, 107. *Warm Winds*, 108. *Path by the Rocks*, 109. *Limbo*, 110. *Sapphire*.

---

9 *Queen of Hearts*, CREATRIX Publishing Line, 1992, Watercolor, 9" x 12".

10 *Spirit Signs*, CREATRIX Publishing Line, 1996, Watercolor, 12" x 18".

11 *Into the Light*, 2009, Oil on Canvas, 26" x 36".

12 *A Different Point of View*, 2010, Oil on Canvas, 24" x 18".

Order Additional Copies of

Painting **Outside the Lines**

and Melissa Harris products at

MELISSAHARRIS.COM

Wholesale Pricing Is Available